VICTORIAN CRITICAL INTERVENTIONS
Donald E. Hall, Series Editor

PROBLEM NOVELS

Victorian Fiction Theorizes the Sensational Self

ANNA MARIA JONES

THE OHIO STATE UNIVERSITY PRESS
Columbus

Library of Congress Cataloging-in-Publication Data

Jones, Anna Maria, 1972–
Problem novels : Victorian fiction theorizes the sensational self / Anna Maria Jones.
    p. cm. — (Victorian critical interventions)
Includes bibliographical references (p.) and index.
ISBN 978-0-8142-1053-6 (alk. paper) — ISBN 978-0-8142-9133-7 (CD-ROM) 1. English
fiction—19th century—History and criticism—Theory, etc. 2. American fiction—19th
century—History and criticism—Theory, etc. 3. Literature—Philosophy. 4. Self in
literature. 5. Sensationalism in literature. I. Title.
PR871.J66 2007
823.'809353—dc22
                2007002659

Cover design by Janna Thompson-Chordas.
Text design and typesetting by Jennifer Shoffey Forsythe.
Type set in Adobe Palatino.
Printed by Thomson-Shore, Inc.

9 8 7 6 5 4 3 2 1

CONTENTS

ACKNOWLEDGMENTS

I t is my pleasure to thank the many friends and colleagues who were willing to work through various versions of the book for, I suspect, imperfect satisfactions. I am grateful to my mentors at the University of Notre Dame who let me read as many insufferable novels (and as insufferably) as I wanted to. Barbara Green, Jay Walton, and Chris Vanden Bossche were unfailingly helpful. I am also beholden to colleagues at Notre Dame who read and reread early drafts with intelligence and good humor: Lauren Ambrose, Skip Thompson, and Sharon Kayfetz Watrous.

I have been fortunate to have the support of some very smart and generous people throughout this project. At the University of Central Florida, Mark Kamrath and Kate Oliver were insightful readers. Dawn Trouard, Blake Scott, and Melody Bowdon offered sage advice during the publishing process. Tom Krise has been a humane chair. My students at UCF deserve my thanks for their intellectual curiosity, savvy, and willingness to tackle "problem novels." They constantly remind me why I love to study Victorian literature. I am grateful to my friends and colleagues at UCF and elsewhere who have provided intellectual community and moral support over the years, especially but not exclusively the following: Beth Ammerman, Adenike Davidson, Spencer Downing, Dan Gates, Cecile Kandl, Tison Pugh, Lisa Roney, and Laura Winkiel. My most heartfelt thanks to Matthew Miller, who is the finest wordsmith and only unicyclist I know. Pat Angley and Christine Doran have been generous colleagues and steadfast friends, without whom my sanity surely would have waned. Words cannot express the debt I owe to Kathy Psomiades, who is the wisest, most forbearing of mentors. Without her unflagging support this book would not have been possible. She is the scholarly and professional ideal to which I aspire.

This project has benefited from the expertise of editors and readers at various stages. Part of chapter 1 first appeared as "'A Victim in Search of a Torturer': Reading Masochism in Wilkie Collins's *No Name*" in *Novel: A Forum on Fiction* 33.2 (Spring 2000). Part of chapter 3 appeared as "Eugenics by Way of Aesthetics: Sexual Selection, Cultural Consumption, and the Cultivated Reader in *The Egoist*" in *LIT: Literature, Interpretation, Theory* 16.2 (Spring 2005). I especially want to thank Donald Hall for his generosity as editor of the Victorian Critical Interventions Series and Sandy Crooms, Maggie Diehl, and the other staff members of The Ohio State University Press for their professionalism and civility. And I am grateful to the book's anonymous readers for the intellectual energy they expended on my behalf. Their incisive comments helped me see the manuscript anew.

Finally, thanks to my parents, Myra Jones, and Frank and Carolyn Jones. They have been consistently supportive, generous, and patient over the years. This book is for them.

Toward a Sensational Theory of Criticism

If [after reading sensation novels] the reader is not prepared to be poisoned, stabbed, blown into the air; to find a skeleton in every cupboard, and a lost will in every drawer; to meet with an inconvenient number of husbands, and a most perplexing superfluity of wives; and to get rid of them by means of arson, strangulation, or a deep well, he must be very insensible indeed to the influence and charm of the situation.

Having prepared us by these well-known arts not to be surprised at anything, our sensational novelists then introduce us to domestic relations of an exceedingly peculiar character. The means are various, though only slightly various, but the end invariably one—to make the reader very tolerant of whatever strange thing may happen beneath the roof of the home to whose secrets he is introduced.

—Alfred Austin, "Our Novels: The Sensational School" (1870)

The reigning contextual mode of critical study of the Victorian period … relies on the fluid translation of a (social, economic, intellectual) environment into fictional discourse: typically, a more-or-less out of the way historical feature of the period is characterized through the selective use of primary and secondary materials, and its pertinence to the proper assessment of (usually canonical) texts asserted. To be sure, there may be side skirmishes with Michel Foucault or Nancy Armstrong in the introduction, but such theoretical anxieties pass, and the critic settles down to read a few canonical and perhaps a smaller number of uncanonical Victorian novels with a mind stocked more-or-less full of writing on, say, sanitation, correcting a few previous readings as he or she goes … That the limits of this mode of criticism, as commonly practiced, are familiar and much discussed makes their persistence all the more intriguing.

—Andrew Miller, "Recent Studies in the Nineteenth Century" (2003)

In his 2003 review essay, Andrew Miller registers dissatisfaction with the year's research in the nineteenth century, which showed a preponderance of Foucault-inspired studies "confidently immured within an orthodox, loosely new-historical set of historiographical assumptions, devoted to understanding and judging individual texts by appeal to historical contexts sometimes richly—but often poorly—conceived" (960). Of this "reigning mode" he goes on to say, perhaps with more accuracy than charity: "At their least successful, such books display a kind of strangled ambition, narrowing their contextual field but making hyperbolic claims within that field" (967).

Nor, as Miller points out, is he the only critic to notice the limitations of this critical mode—they are "familiar and much discussed" (967). Indeed, James Eli Adams notes in *his* 2001 "Recent Studies in the Nineteenth Century" essay: "Many recent accounts of Victorian domesticity have restaged versions of what one might call Foucauldian melodrama: the familiar story of the many-headed Hydra of 'surveillance' violating the sanctity of domestic privacy" (858–59). Similarly, Caroline Levine writes in *The Serious Pleasures of Suspense* (2003): "In the wake of Barthes, Belsey and [D. A.] Miller, it has become something of a commonplace to presume that suspense fiction reinforces stability, activating anxiety about the social world only in order to repress that anxiety in favor of unambiguous disclosures and soothing restorations" (2). And Caroline Reitz, whose own *Detecting the Nation* (2004) undertakes "to challenge the us-them model of panopticism" (xv), comments in a 2004 book review:

> Simon Joyce's *Capital Offenses* is one of a recent crop of very welcome books that takes another look at the question of crime and punishment in Victorian culture, a question that since the late 1980s has come to be dominated by Foucauldian readings of power ... Joyce's book joins works ... which ask the reader to challenge the 'containment thesis' of a certain kind of Foucauldian reading of culture and to explore more complicated, less 'unidirectional' ideas about power. (100)

Reitz goes on to compare Simon Joyce's work to Lauren Goodlad's 2003 *Victorian Literature and the Victorian State*, which has received similar press. For example, Jennifer Ruth, citing Andrew Miller's barbed remarks on post-Foucauldian Victorian studies, writes: "For many of its readers, the value of Lauren Goodlad's new book . . . will be determined by its success in offering a paradigm that can move us, as the title of its first chapter puts it, 'Beyond the Panopticon'" ("Review" 121).[1] Editors Amanda Anderson and Joseph Valente describe their 2002 collection, *Disciplinarity at the Fin de Siècle*, in similar language: "In key respects, the present volume looks to a post-Foucauldian dispensation, keeping its distance from approaches that too easily assimilate bodies of knowledge to techniques of management—whether of the social body, the intellectual field, or the individual person" (8).

According to this critical turn, the problem seems to be that Foucault-inspired studies, in the wake of foundational works like Nancy Armstrong's *Desire and Domestic Fiction* (1987), D. A. Miller's *The Novel and the Police* (1988), and Mary Poovey's *Uneven Developments* (1988), are guilty of erasing difference, reading all texts and contexts into a giant uniform power/knowledge edifice. In other words, the tools with which the master narratives of Enlightenment rationality and psychological "repression" were dismantled have instated a new master narrative—one in which surveillance, discursive knowledge, and discipline invariably produce "docile bodies." If only we could "get past" Foucault—one pictures him occupying (or not?) that room in the tower of the Panopticon—we could reinvigorate a stagnant field of study. What is being offered in place of the "comfortable pessimism" (Anderson and Valente 9) of the containment thesis is the exhilaration of messiness, the promise of more than meets the eye, and more or less explicitly the promise of the return of liberal agency. As Jonah Siegel writes in a 2005 review of David Wayne Thomas's *Cultivating the Victorians* (2004), Thomas "attempts to engage the frequently unspoken, but nevertheless influential notion that the cultivation of the individual is best understood as a mystified subjugation of the self quite contrary to the aspiration for individual agency with which it is often associated" (309).[2]

But, I want to suggest, it is not that "we just can't get past Foucault." (Indeed, by giving Foucault credit for the nuances that literary criticism often erases from his theory, we can see that much of what he says about productive as opposed to repressive power still seems useful.[3]) Rather, this Foucauldian paradigm invites scholars to reiterate over and over again, if not the same arguments then the same generic tropes—tropes that depend paradoxically on mutually exclusive notions of cultural power and critical agency. The notion that nothing is outside of discourse, that power invisibly and inexorably penetrates all aspects of modern life, has been explored and elaborated by a generation of scholars whose invocation of Foucault seems to grant them a "get out of discourse free" card. In other words, studies that describe the intricate workings of power and cultural production on unconscious subjects in Victorian culture do so from a privileged position of critical empowerment and distance that the theoretical underpinnings of the projects would deny.

This critical paradigm operates not just on a hermeneutics of suspicion but, I would argue, on a "hermeneutics of sensation"—a mode of inquiry that depends on (1) the critic's suspicion of a "secret" power at work invisibly in some historical context; (2) the ferreting-out of that secret through the critic's detective work, sifting for textual clues; and (3) the revelation of the secret to a readership attuned to the sensational nuances of the genre. Therefore, the similarities between the two passages I quoted as epigraphs to this chapter—Alfred Austin's satirical description of the sensation novel, any sensation novel, in *Temple Bar,* and Andrew Miller's description of a kind of Victorian scholarship "function machine" (context X + novel Y = critical monograph Z)—arise out of more than an incidental confluence. In describing recent work in nineteenth-century studies, Miller is picking up on the dangers of the sensation genre: in seeking to produce sensations in an increasingly jaded reading public, authors resort to means "various, though only slightly various," (Austin 414) to imagine permutations within the prescriptions of the genre.

I trace the generic tropes of current Victorian scholarship back to Victorian literary sensationalism for two reasons: First, like the sensation novel, Victorian cultural studies seeks to expose the hidden significance of the ordinary—to reveal, in Austin's words, "domestic relations of an exceedingly peculiar character." Second, both sensation novels and Victorian cultural studies—Foucauldian and post-Foucauldian alike—grapple with similarly complex and layered theories of subjectivity. Indeed, as I hope to show, some of the difficulties currently at play in literary scholarship "after Foucault"—in particular the problem of accounting for a subject other than as entirely culturally subjugated without merely returning to optimistic faith in the rational autonomous individual—are explored in the very fiction that was so useful for inaugurating the age of Foucault in the first place.

Like its Gothic predecessors, the sensation novel appeals affectively to its readers, offering opportunities for intense attachments and emotional and visceral responses. As Austin sarcastically points out, the sensation novel demands that its reader be "sensible" to its influences. But, unlike the Gothic, the sensation novel's "charm" resides in its exposure of the lurid secrets hidden in the mundane. In 1982 when Patrick Brantlinger wrote "What Is 'Sensational' about the 'Sensation Novel'?" he articulated the parameters of the genre thus:

> The sensation novel was and is sensational partly because of content: it deals with crime, often murder as an outcome of adultery and sometimes of bigamy, in apparently proper, bourgeois, domestic settings ... The best sensation novels are also, as Kathleen Tillotson points out, "novels with a secret," or sometimes several secrets, in which new narrative strategies were developed to tantalise the reader by withholding information rather than divulging it. (30)

John Sutherland similarly identifies two features that characterized the advent of sensation fiction with the 1859 serialization of *The Woman in White*: the "detective feats" of its protagonists and its "high-impact narrative" ("Wilkie Collins" 75).[4] To this I would add that sensation fiction also engages the reader in a fantasy of knowingness in which suspense and uncertainty anticipate the pleasures of revelation and explanation—murkiness precedes clarity; messiness invites resolution. Moreover, the reader's pleasure in the "novel with a secret" (like *Lady Audley's Secret* or *The Moonstone*, say) inheres in the paradoxical pleasure of being simultaneously "in" the mystery, invited to follow along and glean clues alongside the text's detectives, and outside the text, knowing more than a character "embedded" in the narrative.

The discovery of Foucauldian criticism was the bad news that the reader's comfortable yet exciting position of knowingness outside the text is really one embedded in a disciplinary network of which the text itself is a productive part. But this discovery has occasioned a whole new narrative with a secret, a story that critics of Victorian texts and readers offer to *their* readers—a new fantasy of knowingness, a new pleasure in suspense and revelation. Underpinning these new detective stories is the conviction that we are right to be suspicious, that power—coercive or productive—is ethically suspect and that "resistance" is to be fostered. It is not entirely my intention to argue otherwise, although recently critics like James Kincaid and Rey Chow have done so persuasively.[5] But what I do want to suggest is that disciplinary power *as a concept* has become the means of imagining a cultural space exempt from disciplinary power *as a mechanism*. Of course, anyone who works at a university or other institution will not, I imagine, try to argue that she or he operates in a "discipline-free zone," nor even that her research and publishing are pure intellectual endeavor. But within the rhetorical and epistemological (which is to say, metaphorical) space of academic research, the critic emerges as a figure fantastically imbued with agency. In other words, in the "persistent" iterations of the story of disciplinary power in Victorian culture, critics are also telling the story of their own critical detachment and radical social potential.

Readers will no doubt begin to suspect that I am guilty of engaging in a detective story similar to the ones I reveal in other critics' work. I certainly don't want to disavow my own attachments to sensationalism, but rather to offer a kind of self-reflexive criticism that enjoys its guilt, as it were. Garrett Stewart argues in *Dear Reader:* "The novel always reads rather than merely transmits the prevailing discourses of its day" (276). Following this assertion, I take as a premise that, far from "the mid-Victorian novel flourish[ing] in innocence of theory" (Kendrick 1), novels both articulate and critique theories of culturally embedded subjectivity—in other words, they read themselves being read. And I want to present here literary criticism that reads itself reading the Victorians. It is thus my aim in *Problem Novels* to explore the idea that our critical projects have more in common with the "disciplined" (Victorian) reader of Victorian novels than we generally admit. I maintain that the Victorians were not so sensationally susceptible to discipline as they are often represented as being; nor are we so discipline-resistant as we might hope to be.

I consider works by Wilkie Collins, Anthony Trollope, and George Meredith, written within roughly a twenty-five-year span in the 1860s and 1880s. Although only Collins can be said to be a sensation novelist proper, all three novelists engaged very directly with the concept of sensationalism as a mode of appeal to their readership. In each case I argue that while the author posits a reader who is both culturally embedded and sensationally susceptible, he also explores a methodology for critical engagement with cultural texts, thereby simultaneously theorizing a critically empowered subject.[6] Hence, the title *Problem Novels* indicates my sense that these novels pose problems for their readers by inviting them to consider the process of their own subject formation. And, in turn, I consider how these moments of fictional self-consciousness might offer ways of imagining our own critical endeavors as both affectively invested and critically engaged. Before discussing the novels, however, it will be useful to consider the genre of sensational criticism, after which I will turn to some recent efforts to think past the "disciplinary model" of subject formation and discuss how these might be useful for reading problem novels (and *Problem Novels*).

OUR CRITICS: THE SENSATIONAL SCHOOL

As a storyteller [the detective] defines his superiority, conquering the ostensible criminal by absorbing him and his deviant plot within his own controlling story, defeating his rivals by presenting a convincing narrative of explanation, and even, at times, disempowering his fellow characters and figurative readers by subjecting them to artfully contrived moments of shock and sensational revelation.

—Peter Thoms, *Detection and Its Designs* (1998)

If the Victorian sensation novel is about the revelation of shocking secrets, the pursuit of guilty parties, and detection of hidden crimes, then the project of much Victorian cultural studies scholarship likewise has been concerned with outing "invisible" power relationships, finding disciplinary stratagems where there seem to have been only popular novels, or ladies' magazines, or India shawls. Certainly this shape is very clear in work from the 1980s and '90s by Foucauldian scholars like D. A. Miller, Nancy Armstrong, Mary Poovey, Ann Cvetkovich, and others, who addressed themselves to exploring the ramifications of productive power. As Miller writes, for example, in *The Novel and the Police:* "The turn in *The Moonstone* from a professional detective to lay detection acquires its widest resonance as a parable of the modern policing power that comes to rely less on spectacular displays of repressive force than on intangible networks of productive discipline" (51). Similarly, in *Mixed Feelings* (1992), Cvetkovich argues:

> The image of the beautiful and transgressive [Lady Audley] becomes sensational when we know that she is evil and we both see and don't see her criminality in her appearance … The meaning of the sensation or affect is thus constructed rather than natural, and the representation that produces it can signify both female transgression and its containment. (50)

In other words, Miller and Cvetkovich both argue that the exploration of crime within the novel stages the disciplining of subjects within Victorian culture. Robert Audley in *Lady Audley's Secret*, for instance, investigates the secret past of his uncle's charming new wife and reveals, through the accrual of damning evidence, her lurid crimes and insanity, which, having been sensationally revealed, are then contained, literally in an asylum and figuratively within the resolution of the novel itself.

But here Miller and Cvetkovich write themselves into the role of the detective who has discovered a crime, in this case the invisible disciplinary power of the sensation novel itself. They too will track the novels' secrets, revealing them to their readers clue by significant clue, offering a sensational payoff for those who follow their narratives to conclusion. In these narratives the threat of "productive discipline," having been rendered tangible, will be neutralized. I want to be careful here not to imply that these studies or ones that follow them are necessarily wrong. I think that they offer valuable insights into Victorian texts and contexts. However, in mirroring the very narrative structures that they seek to reveal, they too participate in a kind of invisible disciplining, in this case of Victorian studies. And it is perhaps this "disciplining of the discipline" that accounts for the "persistence" that Andrew Miller notes; the discourse of Victorian studies does indeed, as discourses do, produce subjects in a particular mode.

As Miller observes, the sense in current criticism that it is time to move beyond the revelations of works like *The Novel and the Police* doesn't necessarily lead to a different kind of criticism. I want to examine briefly two recent studies that I would call sensational criticism—Caroline Reitz's *Detecting the Nation* (2004) and Simon Joyce's *Capital Offenses* (2003)—and one study that gets accused of sensationalism, but for slightly different reasons, Caroline Levine's *The Serious Pleasures of Suspense* (2003). Although the first two studies offer noteworthy complications of Foucauldian surveillance and engage very directly with the difficulties of doing Victorian studies post-Foucault, they nonetheless reproduce a kind of surveillance narrative within the structure of their arguments.

Both Reitz's and Joyce's studies are concerned with rereading the figure of the detective outside the model of panoptical power. For example, Reitz, who begins her study of Victorian detective fiction with a critique of Foucault's Panopticon, writes:

> In short, contrary to the logic of the Panopticon, the power of surveillance supplies a vital link between center and periphery as much as it reifies a difference between them. By tracking the power of

surveillance as it emerges in the form of the detective, I intend to challenge the "us-them" model of panopticism presently associated with imperial authority, Victorian national identity, and the figure of the detective. (xxiv–xxv)

Reitz's study complicates what she sees as the uniformity of Foucauldian accounts of surveillance, but the very language of her critical project inadvertently creates an "us-them" dichotomy between the Victorians, whose uses of the detective figure are available for observation and analysis, and herself, the critical scholar who "tracks" the power of surveillance in Victorian culture. Reitz, in taking "a closer look at panopticism" to remedy the "too-tidy explanation of the rise of the detective" in post–*The Novel and the Police* scholarship (xx, xxii), performs a well-known trope of the detective novel, whereby the seemingly watertight explanation of the crime (often provided by the bumbling police or an enthusiastic sidekick) is revealed to be a red herring (by the more-clever detective), and the mystery must be addressed anew.

Joyce, whose work, you will recall, Reitz hails as a welcome corrective to Foucauldian scholarship, undertakes a similarly discursive reading of Victorian texts. He describes the objects of his study as follows:

> London, then, is mapped: in a literal way by surveyors, architects, builders, cartographers; and in more figurative ways by novelists, journalists, sociologists, government investigators. I am primarily concerned here with that latter group of texts, as cultural artifacts that are both distinct from and also an extension of the former. (4)

For Joyce, "mapping" is the thing he is studying, but it also becomes the mode of his own analysis, which gathers together cultural artifacts in order to "*draw* distinctions," to incorporate a "model of reception … [that] *directs us back* to practices of reading and the social formation and spaces within which it occurs." Although Joyce's study is ostensibly opposed to "geography as simply the holding in place of the reading subject, as it might be for a Foucauldian criticism," he nevertheless uses Foucault (and Miller as his proxy) as the fixed points around and against which to draw his "reading *formations*" (5, 6; emphases mine). Further, if Joyce attributes to urban Victorians the "desire for mapping," which, he argues, "would seem natural, given this terrifying displacement of self" and would "allow the larger totality to appear knowable" (3), then surely his own project signifies a similar desire to chart hitherto unrevealed terrain in Victorian crime fiction for his readers. Indeed, in the final lines of *Capital Offenses* Joyce reminds his readers that he has "traced ... important shifts in the cultural representations of crime within a dramatically reconfigured political landscape" (233).

The metaphorical language of "tracking" and "mapping" to describe the critical project is by no means unique to Reitz and Joyce. Rather, it is ubiquitous in scholarly writing and signals what I would call "disavowed panoptic privilege."[7] Interestingly, both Reitz and Joyce make a double move: on the one hand, they imply that previous critics have fallen into a sensation trap by offering their readers lurid stories of hidden disciplinary power; on the other hand, they insist on the messiness and "murkiness" of Victorian culture. In other words, by setting their own work apart from previous accounts, which they allege have been too formulaic in their attachments to the "containment thesis," these critics present a picture of Victorian culture newly reinvested with deviance, complexity, and mystery, and therefore inviting new investigation.

In this way, sensational scholarship posits a triple-layered readership: the susceptible, malleable Victorian reader who was "produced" through the discourses of his or her age; the sensational (and therefore imperfectly critical) Victorianist reader who apprehended some but not all of the mystery from the available clues; and the critically savvy "realist" reader of today who, with the benefit of hindsight, can see what was hidden from the Victorians themselves and from past generations of Victorianists. Thus, for example, Lauren Goodlad claims in *Victorian Literature and the Victorian State* to offer her readers the anachronistically privileged perspective to "view the New Poor Law from within the culture that produced it" (35). One can certainly see how this pattern replicates itself with each new study staking a claim based in some part on the insufficiency of previous work and thereby contracting with readers to provide ever newer and bigger revelations. But, in making this kind of gesture toward "truth," critics belie their sensationalism, or rather, paradoxically, they exhibit "detective feats" and offer "high-impact narrative[s]" based on a newer, more-comprehensive, and more-accurate experience of Victorian literature and culture. As James Eli Adams maintains, the new Victorian studies "offer a more complex, more plausible, and ultimately far more engrossing account" than the familiar "Foucauldian melodrama" (859).[8]

What is interesting about this commitment to faithful representation is that it adopts the same language that the Victorians themselves used to privilege realism over sensationalism. Compare, for example, an 1872 review of Anthony Trollope—in which the reviewer claims that the public, "who eagerly swallowed the sensation poison for a time … [now] knows where to turn for the faithful portraiture of the present which alone it loves to study" (Hoey 400)—with Jonah Siegel's review of David Wayne Thomas's *Cultivating Victorians*, which, Siegel claims, "may be recommended as a soft-spoken yet effective corrective to influential ideas of liberal values that have been more often assumed than clearly established" (309). According to Siegel, Thomas's "gentility of expression" and "commendable tact" are coupled with "extremely responsible and archivally informed case studies of Victorian culture" (310). By adopting this "realist vs. sensational" rhetoric, critics answer the crisis of faith that Andrew Miller articulates when he questions the "intriguing persistence" of Foucault. The answer is this: having learned to see through the sensational appeal of panoptical power, the critical world now knows where to turn for the "faithful portraiture" of realist criticism.

This privileging of realism is illustrated in Peter Garrett's 2005 review of Caroline Levine's *The Serious Pleasures of Suspense*. If, for Siegel, David Wayne Thomas is the Trollope of Victorian studies, then Levine is Garrett's Mary Braddon. Garrett makes the now-familiar gesture "beyond" Foucault. He begins by remarking that recent works in Victorian studies have "loosened the hold of notions like Barthes's 'classic realist text' or Foucault's panoptic discipline, enabling us to set aside condescending or suspicious assumptions that nineteenth-century realism was hopelessly naïve or enthralled to bourgeois ideology" (490). He argues, however, that while Levine "presents her study as a contribution to this reappraisal," her "curious" version of realism ultimately undermines the validity of her argument. Garrett concludes, "If Levine had recognized the implausible results of her own critical experiment, and abandoned the effort to link realism with suspense, there would still remain much of interest … But as an account of the relation between 'Victorian realism and narrative doubt,' her book is as implausible as the most sensational fiction" (490–91).

Garrett's invocation of sensation fiction as an uncomplimentary comparison designates Levine's book as sensational because it reveals realism's "secret" attachment to suspense, a secret that he finds far-fetched. Garrett points to the implausibility of sensation

criticism much in the way that Wilkie Collins, perhaps disingenu-
ously, rebuked sensation novelists for the "publication of books that
pander to morbid delight in scenes of crime and guilt, which seem
to have a special attraction to uneducated and debased minds" and
which are "written to gratify a craving after excitement" ("Art of
Novel Writing" 392). According to Collins, and Garrett seemingly,
the sensational author resorts to far-fetched plot devices in order to
pander to his or her audience. Although one would hesitate to suggest that Garrett accuses fellow scholars of possessing "uneducated
and debased minds," I don't think we should overlook the sensational appeal of precisely the implausibility that he rebukes, even in
the most "responsible and archivally informed" of scholarship.

Indeed, the merits of Levine's book or the accuracy of Garrett's
description of it aside, the review itself would seem to occasion at
least two widely divergent responses from readers unfamiliar with
Levine's work. On the one hand, one might say, "Thank goodness
I have been warned away from the implausibilities that this study
would inflict on me," and look for a less sensational study of realism. But on the other hand, one might say, "'Implausible as the most
sensational fiction?' You say that like it's a bad thing!" and run over
to the campus library first thing to investigate.[9] I would suggest that
despite current disavowals of sensationalism, the "implausible"
argument is precisely what is prized in Victorian studies, and with
good reason. After all, as every reader of sensation novels knows, the
most obvious explanation is never the right answer. The pleasure of
uncovering the hidden significance of a seemingly inconsequential
clue is much the same, I would argue, whether one is reading about
Walter Hartright discovering the importance of a railway timetable
to Laura Fairlie's "death," or about Nancy Armstrong unearthing
the pivotal role of conduct literature in the formation of bourgeois
ideology, or about Caroline Reitz revealing the English detective at
the outskirts of the Empire.

In fact, what I find most interesting about Levine's work is that
in linking the unlikely suspects of serious intellectual skepticism and
narrative suspense, she shows how cultural studies scholarship has
inherited the intertwined legacies of critical inquiry and narrative
pleasure from a Victorian hermeneutics of suspicion, thereby highlighting her readers' own critical investments even as she explores
Victorian attachments to suspense. As she says: "Suspenseful narratives teach us to take pleasure in the very activity of stopping to

doubt our most entrenched beliefs, waiting for the world to reveal its surprises, its full unyielding otherness. The pleasures of suspense are, then, remarkably serious pleasures" (10). As an extension of this, I would suggest that the payoff for reading Victorian scholarship (for Victorianists) is not just the professional satisfaction of acquiring accurate and comprehensive knowledge; it is also the pleasures of narrative suspense and revelation, of participating in fantasies of critical agency. And if this is true, then the answer to the persistent problem of the "sensational Foucault" is not to embrace a "realist" mode of criticism as somehow truer and less problematic, or more "tasteful." Rather, we should acknowledge (in order to explore) our attachments to the sensational genre. What are the stakes for the critic who appeals sensationally to his or her audience by offering the "implausible" argument? Or who writes, for example, for a series that offers its readers "brief manuscripts that make brash and revisionary claims"?[10] Or for the critic who deprecates the sensational in criticism? The main question to ask may not be, how should we read the Victorians? but rather, what are we like when we read the Victorians?

EXPLORING AMBIVALENT AGENCY

If recent critiques of Foucault's disciplinary model have tended to reproduce some of the same sensational tropes that they uncover, some have also explored useful ways to reinvest the disciplined subject with agency. In her essay "The Temptations of Aggrandized Agency: Feminist Histories and the Horizon of Modernity" (2000), Amanda Anderson considers problems that arise within Foucauldian scholarship. She argues provocatively that Foucauldian notions of cultural power have led to a kind of theoretical conundrum for studies like Nancy Armstrong's *Desire and Domestic Fiction* and Mary Poovey's *Uneven Developments*, wherein

> agency is imagined as continuous with the unreflective forms of power that are simply transmitted by culturally embedded subjects. Yet on the other hand, strange exceptions occur, wherein certain historical subjects are exempted from the networks of power, and consequently granted what I will characterize as "aggrandized agency," which is marked by both critical lucidity and political potency. (44)

Anderson points to particular figures, like the Brontës for Armstrong and Florence Nightingale for Poovey, who, unlike the run of feminine subjects who are unconscious of their participation in or subjection to cultural power, are granted a political savvy and insight into the workings of disciplinary power that matches that of the critic herself. As Anderson points out: "On one level these critics are skeptical that any such detachment is possible, yet on another level they rely on such detachment for the promulgation of their critical social theories" (52).

The difficulty, as Anderson identifies it, is one of theorizing cultural power and critical agency in a way that, on the one hand, takes into account the ubiquity (and complexity) of modern power and, on the other hand, allows for the possibility of culturally embedded subjects engaging with and critiquing forms of power in self-conscious ways. Anderson argues that we need to pay careful attention to the ways in which the Victorians (and we as their descendants) cultivate an ambivalent relationship to ideals of detachment. She concludes: "The cultivation of detachment—which in some sense is only another name for the examined life—is always an ongoing, partial project, whose interrelated ethical and epistemological dimensions promote the reflexive interrogation of norms and the possibility for individual and collective self-determination" (63).[11]

This is the same issue that Judith Butler explores in *The Psychic Life of Power*, in which she contends:

> A critical analysis of subjection involves: (1) an account of the way regulatory power maintains subjects in subordination by producing and exploiting the demand for continuity, visibility, and place; (2) recognition that the subject produced as continuous, visible and located is nevertheless haunted by an inassimilable remainder, a melancholia that marks the limits of subjectivation; (3) an account of the iterability of the subject that shows how agency may well consist in opposing and transforming the social terms by which it is spawned … The analysis of subjection is always doubled, tracing the conditions of subject formation and tracing the turn against those conditions for the subject—and its perspective—to emerge. (29)

Butler uses the psychoanalytic concept of melancholia to imagine a culturally embedded subject that is, although brought into being by power, not fully accounted for by its subjection. She calls this the "double-bind of agency"—a paradox whereby the subject, which is a product of power, resists the very thing to which it owes its existence.

Given Anderson's ongoing critique of Butler's version of the performative subject, my juxtaposition of the two may seem idiosyncratic. In particular, Anderson criticizes what she sees as Butler's inability to account for intersubjective and collective agency.[12] Yet I think the two offer similar, and similarly useful, articulations of subjectivity "in process." Like Anderson's description of the "ongoing, partial project" of critical detachment, Butler's emphasis on this double-bind, or ambivalence, wherein the "subject is *neither* fully determined by power *nor* fully determining of power (but significantly and partially both)" (17), accounts for the notion of the subject as *becoming* rather than simply *being*. That is to say, rather than existing in any self-evident way (either as autonomous rational being, or as hapless subject to disciplinary power), one is always in the process of becoming, which, as Butler insists, allows for "the possibility of a re-embodying of the subjectivating norm that can redirect its normativity" (99). This makes novels, with their virtually endless iterability, their demands for affective investments, and their own deep investments in social systems, seem like particularly apt instances to examine the subject's "reiteration or rearticulation of itself as a subject" (99). It is this notion of ambivalent agency that I attempt to keep at the forefront as I examine the novels in this study.

As I mentioned earlier, I find the novels of the mid-nineteenth century particularly concerned with theorizing "problematic" versions of subjectivity. This is not to say that one wouldn't find a species of ambivalent agency in an eighteenth-century Gothic novel like *The Monk* or a modernist novel like *Orlando*. Indeed, my argument may be more generically than historically specific. Nevertheless, at the risk of slipping into the "reigning contextual mode of criticism," I would suggest that the fierce debates in the 1850s through the 1880s surrounding the legislation of married women's property forced a crisis in Victorians' understanding of individual agency, and it is this crisis that plays out in the theoretical texts that I call "problem novels." As Barbara Leigh Smith Bodichon explains in 1854, the Victorian social and legal system treated single and married women very differently: "A single woman has the same rights to property, to protection from the law, and has to pay the same taxes to the State, as a man," but in marriage

> a man and wife are one person in the law; the wife loses all her rights as a single woman, and her existence is entirely absorbed in that of her husband. He is civilly responsible for her acts; she lives under his protection or cover, and her condition is called coverture ... A woman's body belongs to her husband; she is in his custody, and he can enforce his right by a writ of *habeas corpus*. (3, 6)[13]

Whereas a single woman could earn and keep money, enter into contracts, sue and be sued, once she chose to enter into a marriage contract she lost the ability to do all of these on her own behalf. Indeed, under coverture a woman could not be convicted of stealing from her husband, because it would be impossible to steal from oneself. In other words, a single woman who had "attained her majority," who was in possession of her own wealth and person, could exercise her autonomy in order to enter into a marriage contract, under which contract she would forfeit the existence of that autonomous self. Woman, therefore, represented *both* a figure profoundly beholden to the forces of her subjection and an agent in excess of that subjection—a figure, in other words, ideally situated to embody subjectivity "in process."

Given the Victorian woman's ambivalent agency, then, it is not surprising that marriage in many a mid-Victorian novel would present a problem as much as a resolution. The novels that I discuss here engage with this dilemma of ambivalent agency on two levels. First, they explore the "contingent" nature of agency that can be both exercised within and erased by social interactions within their plots. In novels like Wilkie Collins's *No Name*, Anthony Trollope's *Can You Forgive Her?*, and George Meredith's *Diana of the Crossways,* the active, willful heroines are a far cry from the victim-heroines of novels like *Clarissa* and *The Monk,* or even the "virtue rewarded" heroines of *Pamela* and *Mansfield Park.* Instead these novels feature heroines (and sometimes heroes) who make perverse choices, who commit themselves to dangerous courses or eschew happy endings, or who actively pursue or resist their own disciplining. And, second, for all of these novels, the consideration of readerly affect and subjection occurs at the interstices of genre, where novels play with their own conventions or invoke their own relationship to genre as a rhetorical gesture. Through generically self-conscious plots, the novels explore the reader's vexed agency, asking what it means for a reader to choose to both accept and critique (critique while accepting) the discipline of the novel.

In chapter 1, "Sensation Fiction Theorizes Masochism," I consider how mid-Victorian notions of the contract enabled novels to articulate ambivalent agency. I argue that the view of the contract, which Henry Sumner Maine asserted in his 1861 treatise *Ancient Law* was the foremost distinguishing feature of "civilized" society, allows widely disparate writers in the 1860s, Wilkie Collins and John Ruskin, to theorize the construction of a masochistic subject through affective investments in painful reading. In contractual exchange, the law of the family, inheritance, and the father's legacy are supplanted by relationships forged between individuals and based on mutual obligation. Power and position are no longer only inherited, but can be mobile. Whereas Ruskin's two lectures "Of Kings' Treasuries" and "Of Queens' Gardens," which *Sesame and Lilies* (1865) comprises, call for readers to "annihilat[e] our own personality" (43) in order to become better selves, Collins's two novels *No Name* (1862) and *Armadale* (1866) enact this dynamic both within the novels' plots and as a narrative contract between novel and reader—that is, the act of reading is posited as an agreement to suffer. Thus the authors imagine the possibilities for an active, contracting subject, one who does not capitulate unquestioningly to institutional power so much as engage with it, even manipulate it for his or her desired results—a knowing, albeit disciplined, subject for whom the processes of subject production, regulation, and control are at all times visible, explicit, and, most importantly, imbued with a kind of painful pleasure. I argue that this preoccupation with the willingness of characters and readers to suffer suggests a way of rethinking the productive nature of the reader's affective investments—it offers masochism as a position from which submission and self-consciousness are possible simultaneously.

If one of the promises of late-Victorian realism is to debunk the untruths and exaggerations of sensation fiction, then seemingly the adoption of economic language—the metaphor of the "marriage market," for example—to describe sexual relationships is part of the process of demystification. This rhetorical conflation of economics and sexuality has led, in large part, to the current critical emphasis on the realist novel's status as a commodity as well. However, as I argue in chapter 2, "Realism Theorizes Speculative Investments," the adoption of economic language to describe sexual relationships shows that the Victorians themselves understood that *both* the economic system and the sexual system were dependent on emotionally laden choices, sensational payoffs, symbolic exchanges. This is the problem for realist fiction: one of the "truths" about the way the system works is that in order for the system to work, the truth must be disavowed—sensational investments are in fact indispensable to the functioning of sexual exchanges, just as speculative investments are indispensable to the functioning of the financial system. The three Anthony Trollope novels discussed in this chapter—*The Struggles of Brown, Jones, and Robinson* (1862), *Can You Forgive Her?* (1864), and *Miss Mackenzie* (1865)—explore the novelist's role as a producer of belief in the system of sexual exchange. Moreover, they highlight the contradictory obligations of the reader of realist fiction—simultaneously to invest and to resist investment in the romance.

In the late-Victorian imagination, rhetoric of aesthetic valuation became linked to social-evolutionary progress. For cultural and evolutionary theorists, refinement of public taste not only signified but also *produced* social progress, just as lack of refinement impeded it. Thus, in chapter 3, "The 'New Fiction' Theorizes Cultural Consumption," I examine this intersection of aesthetic standards and social (d)evolution in two novels by George Meredith, *The Egoist* (1879) and *Diana of the Crossways* (1885), alongside his 1877 aesthetic manifesto, *An Essay on Comedy;* Matthew Arnold's cultural criticism in *Culture and Anarchy* (1869) and "The Function of Criticism at the Present Time" (1864); and Francis Galton's foundational eugenics treatise, *Hereditary Genius* (1869). Meredith, in both *An Essay* and his novels, imagines the woman reader as crucially linked to the evolution or degeneration of civilization, depending on the extent to which her cultural taste can be educated. He insists on "Comedy" as the antidote to sentimentality and sensationalism in literature and as the key to social progress. If Comedy is the critical lens through which to address society's foibles, however, it is also a generic structure dependent on sentimental and romantic tropes. Coupling the self-consciously sensationalized romance with social critique grounded in theories of sexual selection and cultural evolution, *The Egoist* and *Diana of the Crossways* ridicule the sentimental reader's affective attachments to the domestic comedy, yet also encourage complicity with the very sentimentalism they deride, thereby producing a layered analysis of the reader's responsibility in civilization's progress.

I argue that this stress on the responsibility of the "cultivated" reader still resonates in literary studies today as the critic's fantasy of omnipotence—that is, that solely or primarily through the intellectual transmission from critical author (cultural authority) to student/reader may civilization evolve, paradigms shift, and oppressive power structures be resisted. But Meredith's understanding of Comedy also tells us to pay attention to how we have been "mixing our private interests" (*An Essay* 36) with the object of our observation, thereby offering us a way to own our sensational attachments even as we strive for the ideal of critical acuity.

And thus, "my present design being to rouse the reader's interest" (Collins, *No Name* 6) in the following chapters—all of which consider the question of genre as they reflect on the limits of readerly investments—I invite my readers to consider their own investments (and my own investments) in *this* sensational genre too.

CHAPTER ONE

Sensation Fiction
Theorizes Masochism

Having then faithfully listened to the great teachers, that you may enter into their Thoughts, you have yet this higher advance to make;—you have to enter into their Hearts. Passion, or "sensation." I am not afraid of the word; still less of the thing. You have heard many outcries against sensation lately; but, I can tell you, it is not less sensation we want, but more. The ennobling difference between one man and another,—between one animal and another,—is precisely in this, that one feels more than another. If we were sponges, perhaps sensation might not be easily got for us; if we were earth-worms, liable at every instant to be cut in two by the spade, perhaps too much sensation might not be good for us. But being human creatures, IT IS good for us; nay, we are only human in so far as we are sensitive, and our honour is precisely in proportion to our passion.

—John Ruskin, "Of Kings' Treasuries" (1864)

Critics have been wont to emphasize the sensation novel's preoccupation with mystery and detection, with the quarry of dangerous femininity sounded and exposed by the indefatigable detective/hunter. As I discussed in the introduction, the sensation genre so conceived provided the foundation for some of the first and most influential articulations of the productive hypothesis of power in Victorian studies. D. A. Miller, for example, asserts in *The Novel and the Police* that the very fictional representation of a mystery that must be discovered is in itself an exercise of a disciplinary power: "To the extent that the genre of the novel *belongs* to the disciplinary field that it portrays, our attention needs to go beyond the policing forces represented in the novel to focus on what Foucault might call the 'micro-politics' of novelistic convention" (21).[1] Through readings of the sensation novel like Miller's we have become proficient in uncovering the discursive significance of the sensation novel whose secrets are systematically revealed and luridly detailed—simultaneously titillating with the spectacle of transgression and reassuring with the exercise of disciplinary power over that transgression. Within this framework the detective occupies the position of the disciplinarian, and the possessor of the secret becomes the docile subject described by Foucault in *Discipline and Punish*.[2] These analyses are based on the assumption that the reader's desire lies with the disciplinary gaze that can uncover and render legible the secret crimes.

Whereas I would agree that this model works for a great many sensation narratives, I believe that it fails to explain fully the ways in which other sensation novels engage in the production of subjectivities. As the epigraph from "Of Kings' Treasuries" suggests, sensationalism is also about willing submission to the text, about agreeing to subject oneself to the "discipline" of reading. Thus, while many sensation plots may be impelled by the reader's identification with the detective and his or her pursuit of the hidden "truth," some notable exceptions rely instead on the reader's investment in the object of that discipline. Without denying the pleasure that comes from occupying the position, alongside the detective, of voyeur and disciplinarian, I focus in this chapter on a very different textual pleasure—a masochistic identification with the hunted, and ultimately disciplined, transgressive subject. The novels that I deal with here, *No Name* and *Armadale*, start with the revelation of a secret that negates from the beginning the sanctity of the domestic sphere and the innocence of its inhabitants. Because the secret is revealed to the reader but not to the detectives within the novel, the reader's investment becomes aligned with the transgressor, the possessor of the secret.

I argue that this structure invites the reader to occupy, with the protagonist, a masochistic relationship to disciplinary power. And, far from questioning the power of detection, the structure depends upon the inevitability of discipline (and punishment) for the masochistic pleasure of holding a secret. As the narrator informs us in *No Name:*

> Nothing is this world is hidden for ever. The gold which has lain for centuries unsuspected in the ground, reveals itself one day on the surface. Sand turns traitor, and betrays the footstep that has passed over it; water gives back to the tell-tale surface the body that has been

drowned. Fire leaves the confession, in ashes, of the substance consumed in it. Hate breaks the prison-secrecy in the thoughts, through
the doorway of the eyes; and Love finds the Judas who betrays it
with a kiss. Look where we will, the inevitable law of revelation
is one of the laws of nature: the lasting preservation of a secret is a
miracle the world has never yet seen. (34)

Given the futility of secret-keeping, the whole plot of *No Name*—
describing the attempts of the heroine, Magdalen, through elaborate
disguises and deceits to regain her father's lost fortune—must end
in Magdalen's failure and discovery. Our identification with Magdalen, therefore, must be vexed by our knowledge of her ultimate
defeat. Furthermore, the entire plot is colored by the heroine's *own*
understanding that what she is doing puts her beyond the protection
of the law and legitimate friends. She too sees her quest as doomed
to failure. As she pronounces to her cohort, the swindler Captain
Wragge: "I have lost all care for myself. I have only one end in life
now; and the sooner I reach it—and die—the better" (338).[3] Magdalen is rewarded precisely because she "loses all care" for herself,
because she mortifies herself, inviting rather than avoiding the pain
of punishment.

Similarly, in *Armadale*, not only is the reader privy to all the
secrets in the novel, but the hero (one of four Allan Armadales) finds
redemption and a new life by relinquishing his power and agency.
He gives up his inheritance and his name, assuming the alias Ozias
Midwinter in order to become the faithful "dog" of the man who is
by birthright his rival. Both Magdalen and Midwinter exercise their
agency to engage in complex negotiations with disciplinary power.
No Name and *Armadale* imagine that the protagonist's self-realization
can be effected, however paradoxically, only through the annihila-
tion of the self.

In imagining this paradoxical self-realization through annihila-
tion these novels participate in a kind of masochistic logic on two
levels: first, as a mechanism of narrative logic *within* the text, when
the characters participate in their own subjection, and, second, as a
tool for the reader to participate in his or her own subjection *by* the
text. I argue that in inviting the reader to participate in these stories
of ambivalent agency, the texts are theorizing themselves and the
act of reading as intricately connected to mid-nineteenth-century
culture's emerging social possibilities for individual self-fashioning.
Before considering the historical specificities of Victorian masochistic

reading, however, it will be useful to reflect on masochism as it has been articulated in current critical discussions.

HOW MASOCHISM WORKS (AND HOW IT DOESN'T)

Masochism offers a tantalizing framework for critics to theorize subversive agency; as a perverse enactment of the subject's relationship to power, deconstructing the pleasure/pain binary, masochism seems cunningly seditious. Yet it has proven elusive as a tool of the revolution. Two problems have plagued theoretical annexing of masochism as subversion: the problem of gender and the problem of the "real" vs. the parodic. As we will see, these two are intertwined. John Noyes, in his insightful *The Mastery of Submission* (1997), situates contemporary critical discussions of masochism in the nineteenth-century "invention" of two kinds of masochistic body. As he writes:

> The masochist's body was invented in the late nineteenth century as a machine that could do one of two things, depending on how it was regarded, how it was used, or where it was positioned. It could reduce socially nonproductive aggressivity to an individual pathology, or it could transform social control into sexual pleasure. The one use of the masochist's body supports the project of socially sanctioned aggression and the various stereotypes society has developed in order to invest cultural identity with aggressivity. The other use of the masochist's body subverts this project, initiating an unsettling process whereby cultural identity is parodied, masqueraded, and appropriated in the name of pleasure. These two uses initiate all the conflicts surrounding masochism as we understand it today. (9–10)

It is not, I think, too much of an overstatement to say that these two uses of masochism have been gendered for critics and proponents of masochism: the normative, socially sanctioned kind attached to feminine interpellation, the "unsettling" parodic kind attached to masculine perversion.[4] Partially this paradox arises as far back as Freud's "The Economic Problem of Masochism" (1924), in which he describes the masochistic fantasy as placing "the subject in a characteristically female situation ... that is, being castrated, or copulated with, or giving birth to a baby" (277). In other words, normative, heterosexual, female experience constitutes the perverse fantasies of the male masochist. Within this structure, there is no room to imagine a female perversion that might be called masochistic; women are by definition masochists.

Following this logic, feminist literary critics have tended to elide the terms *femininity, passivity,* and *masochism,* thereby reading scenes of female suffering as inevitably satisfying some sinister, masculine-identified "gaze." For example, in *Schools of Sympathy* (1997) Nancy Roberts describes the role of suffering protagonists such as Clarissa and Tess thus:

> The "heroism" or "greatness" of the heroine is measured by means other than her actions. For she can *do,* can *move,* very little. (After all, as victim she is less an actor than one who is acted upon.) Her heroism is measured instead by the pity and sympathy she elicits from others, by the extent to which she *moves* them (us) ... [She] is placed as an icon, the purpose of which is to draw and invite our response. Often she is represented as having little life or character of her own. (6)

Similarly, in *In the Name of Love* (1992) Michelle Massé describes masochism as one of the primary facts of women's acculturation:

> Masochism is the end result of a long and varyingly successful cultural training. This training leaves its trace upon individual characters and upon the Gothic itself, which broods upon its originating trauma, the denial of autonomy or separation for women, throughout the centuries ... Girls who, seeking recognition and love, learn to forget or deny that they also want independence and agency, grow up to become women who are Gothic heroines. (3)

Even more nuanced arguments about female suffering, like Ann Cvetkovich's chapter on *East Lynne* in *Mixed Feelings,* tend to erase the agency of victimized heroines. In this way, masochism becomes the big blank of passivity, of status quo, of the lack of radical potential for women.[5]

Yet even the "good" kind of masochism—parodic, perverse, and subversive—runs into trouble, for the pleasurable pain of the masochistic fantasy, it turns out, is really real pain, and thus, as Noyes says, "Masochism is a continuation of social violence" (14). This is a problem that Slavoj Žižek poses in his 2003 essay "The Masochistic

Social Link," in which he uses the film *Fight Club* to consider masochism as revolutionary social praxis:

> Is then the very idea of the "fight club," the evening encounters of
> men who play the game of beating up each other, not the very model
> of such a false transgression/excitation, of the impotent *passage à
> l'acte* that bears witness to the failure to intervene effectively in the
> social body? Does *Fight Club* not stage an exemplary case of the
> *inherent transgression:* far from effectively undermining the capitalist
> system, does it not enact the obscene underside of the "normal"
> capitalist subject? (120)

If masochism perpetuates the forms and the outcomes of social regulation and subjection, how can it also instigate a revolutionary break
with oppressive social formations?

In several recent articles, John Kucich has suggested that the way
around this impasse is to conceive of masochism outside of a Freud-
ian-Lacanian "oedipal" tradition, which, he says, "severely limits
cultural and political interpretation" ("Melancholy Magic" 365). He
argues instead that relational psychology's model of a preoedipal
and nonsexualized masochism offers a way to explain, in particular,
"the central role that masochism played in shaping the ideological
structures of Victorian middle-class culture" (365). Kucich's appli-
cation of relational psychology offers its most direct challenge to
psychoanalytic discussions of masochism, but his work can also be
read as part of the current attempts in Victorian scholarship to move
beyond Foucault. He calls to account cultural critics who "regard
[masochism] as general trope for power relations," declaring that
even these "tend to preserve the oedipal oppositions of dominance
and submission—along with the thematics of punishment, forbidden desire, and potentially subversive abjection—that characterize
the oedipal narrative" ("Olive Schreiner" 83). As an antidote to these
totalizing models, Kucich claims, relational psychology "reimagines
many sites of conceptual ordering besides binary hierarchies of
power, and it addresses a wide variety of intersubjective conflicts"
(83).

Although it is not quite clear how "intersubjective conflicts" might
be separated from "hierarchies of power," Kucich offers a salutary
warning to critics of masochism not to fall into the trap of universal-
izing oedipal logic as either a psychological fact or as a metaphor for
social power, but instead to see masochism as participating in and

enabling an array of social interactions. However, in considering Victorian masochistic logic, we should not be too quick to throw the Daddy out with the bathwater, as it were. By dismissing the oedipal component of masochism, we are not just freeing analysis from the "leftover" of a Freudian master narrative, but rather eliding the very real political and social component of the "law of the father" that structured so many Victorian relationships. What I mean is that the mid-nineteenth-century culture, in which the masochist-as-subject position was so widely articulated, was a culture that understood itself as standing in an increasingly vexed relationship to the code of primogeniture and the structuring principles of patrilineal inheritance and as moving toward a social system in which individual agency was mobilized through economic and juridical invocations of the contract.[6]

This is why Gilles Deleuze's now-classic essay "Coldness and Cruelty" is still important for theorists who wish to account for masochism's complexities. Deleuze emphatically separates masochism from sadism, aligning masochism with contracts and sadism with institutions. He describes the masochist in this manner:

> We are no longer in the presence of a torturer seizing upon a victim and enjoying her all the more because she is unconsenting and unpersuaded. We are dealing instead with a victim in search of a torturer and who needs to educate, persuade and conclude an alliance with the torturer in order to realize the strangest of schemes. This is why ... the masochist draws up contracts while the sadist abominates them and destroys them. The sadist is in need of institutions, the masochist of contractual relations. (20)

The masochistic contract requires punishment, suffering, and sacrifice, but most important, it demands agency. Passive suffering alone is not enough—one must consent to, *contract* to suffer.

Thus, Henry Sumner Maine's articulation—in his 1861 treatise, *Ancient Law*—of the centrality of the contract to modern society sheds light on how masochism might be both politically and socially "real" and also fundamentally connected to the "oedipal fantasy":

> There are few general propositions concerning the age to which we belong which seem at first to be received with readier concurrence than the assertion that the society of our day is mainly distinguished from that of preceding generations by the largeness of the sphere

which is occupied in it by Contract ... Not many of us are so unob-
servant as not to perceive that in innumerable cases where old law
fixed a man's position irreversibly at his birth, modern law allows
him to create it for himself by convention. (252)

For Maine the contract replaces primogeniture; the law of the family,
inheritance, and the father's legacy is supplanted by relationships
forged between individuals and based on mutual obligation. Power
and position are no longer only inherited, but can be mobile.[7] Relationships are not fixed, but can be negotiated, insofar as the law of
the father can be circumvented.

This understanding of the contract, moreover, was particularly
pertinent to the Victorians' exploration of the "Woman Question"
and married women's property laws. In language very similar to
Maine's, Frances Power Cobbe argues that granting women the same
rights to contract as men makes sense only in a "modern" (English)
society:

> There is no use reverting .... to old Eastern, or classic, or feudal rela-
> tions between men and women ... As the ages of force and violence
> have passed away, and as more and more room has been left for
> the growth of gentler powers, women (especially in England) have
> gradually and slowly risen to a higher place. ("Criminals" 125)

And she concludes even more forcefully: "As for civil rights—the
right to hold property, to make contracts, to sue and be sued—no
class, however humble, stupid, and even vicious, has ever been denied
them since serfdom and slavery came to an end" (128). Woman's
interstitial position between serfdom and civil enfranchisement—her
radically different status as *femme sole* or *femme covert*—made her,
perhaps, ideally suited to masochism; however, I would suggest this
is not, as critics like Michelle Massé have argued, because she was
(only) a victim of cultural forces but because she was a subject whose
agency could be exercised to relinquish agency. I don't mean to
imply that real Victorian women weren't oppressed by real material
and financial exigencies wherein the "choice" to marry was a often
grim nonchoice, but I do want to assert that the imaginative force of
the masochistic contract meant that portrayals of women's agency
and women's suffering meant more than just their oppression.[8] The
"Woman Question" debates that raged throughout the latter decades
of the nineteenth century meant that Woman called into question

the process by which one came to be a subject and what exactly that subjectivity might entail.

Being able to contract means that one has some limited power over one's subjectivity. In other words, it means that one can, to a certain extent, choose the ways in which one interacts with disciplinary power. The question then is not, can one escape a subordinate relationship to disciplinary authority?—one can't—but, *how* does one occupy that subordinate position? Masochism demands, as a precondition, a certain amount of agency that can be exercised in choosing one's subjection. The exercise of agency, even to suffer or relinquish agency, is, to quote Slavoj Žižek, "its own ontological proof, an immediate index of its own truth" (122). This means that as an active, contracting subject, the masochist engages with disciplinary power, even manipulates it, for his or her desired results. Thus, the masochist becomes, in a way not anticipated by Bentham's Panopticon, a knowing, albeit disciplined, subject for whom the processes of subject production, regulation, and control are at all times visible, explicit, and even eroticized. The contract is the site of that visibility—the articulation of the subject's relationship to and under the law.

We might think of the contract, therefore, in terms of Judith Butler's notion of ambivalent agency. The reiterations of contractual obligation highlight the "temporal paradox" of subjectivity, to understand which, according to Butler, "we must lose the perspective of a subject already formed in order to account for our own becoming. That 'becoming' is no simple or continuous affair but an uneasy practice of repetition and its risks, compelled yet incomplete, wavering on the horizon of social being" (30). Sensationalism was just such an uneasy literary and disciplinary practice, which provided the Victorians with the means to view their own "horizon of social being." In the following section, I will argue that John Ruskin's *Sesame and Lilies* theorizes a subject of ambivalent agency, willfully submissive to the discipline of reading.

SESAME AND LILIES: "ANNIHILATING OUR OWN PERSONALITY"

You will see that most men's minds are indeed little better than rough heath wilderness, neglected and stubborn, partly barren, partly overgrown with pestilent brakes, and venomous, wind-sown herbage of evil surmise; that the first thing you have to do

for them, and for yourself, is eagerly and scornfully set fire to this; burn all the jungle
into wholesome ash-heaps, and then plough and sow. All the true literary work before
you, for life, must begin with obedience to that order, "Break up your fallow ground,
and sow not among thorns."

—John Ruskin, "Of Kings' Treasuries" (1865)

The Victorians often characterized reading as unconscious consumption. In language remarkably similar to Foucauldian critiques of power, Victorian debates about the dangers of reading describe malleable readers, highly susceptible to the affective appeals of fiction. As one antisensation critic writes in 1866:

> We do not for a moment mean to say that the authors who appear to think that a tale would not be complete unless it contained a bigamy, an elopement, and a murder ... would advise their fair readers to imitate the examples of those extraordinary heroines who they are so fond of depicting, the beautiful women of elegant figure and golden locks, whose fascinating exterior only hides a subtle brain and pitiless heart ... But we do say that it is impossible to cultivate extensively this kind of acquaintance—to have the mind engaged and the feelings interested in the plots and machinations of these ruthless schemers, to be almost unconsciously drawn in the habit of regarding such crimes as being neither very exceptional nor very monstrous,—without having the moral nature degraded. ("Recent Novels" 104)[9]

Here the insidious power of the texts lies in their ability to engage minds and interest feelings without conscious acquiescence on the reader's part. And, as critics have noted, this expression of sensation fiction's dangerous potential is connected to the Victorians' shifting understanding of the mind-body link, whereby excessive mental agitation could instigate physical illness, and vice versa.[10]

Without denying the strength of affective or sensational appeals, however, other articulations of the process of reading challenged the unconsciousness of the reader. For example, in an 1870 article in *Tinsley's Magazine*, "The Uses of Fiction," the unnamed author argues, on the one hand, that the merits of a fictional romance may be best judged by a young girl reader whose "experiences [of romance] ... have rendered her sensitive and appreciative on this one point," and, on the other hand, that this same young girl reader will be able to judge the merits of her real-life romances because "long before she enter[s] upon these experiences herself, she ha[s] read accounts of how other people encountered them" (6–7). The author imagines the girl reader both formed by and also acutely critical of her reading experiences.[11]

In "Of Kings' Treasuries," the first of two essays on reading that *Sesame and Lilies* comprises, John Ruskin describes sensationalism as the reader's willing submission to the discipline of the text. Critical attention to *Sesame and Lilies* has often focused on Ruskin's delineation of the "separate spheres" for women and men, particularly in the second essay, "Of Queens' Gardens," which addresses women readers and their responsibilities. I want to focus primarily on how Ruskin articulates a mode of masochistic self-fashioning through sensational reading, although, as I will demonstrate, Ruskin conceives of that sensational masochism differently for men and women in the two essays.

It is certainly not my intention here to imply that Ruskin was really a champion of the sensation novel. But I do want to suggest that Ruskin's description of reading as a "harrowing" discipline illustrates how Victorians understood the masochism of reading. Ruskin was critical of popular fiction, precisely because it could engage the reader too much. He argues the point in "Of Queens' Gardens":

> With respect to the sore temptation of novel reading, it is not the badness of the novel that we should dread, so much as its over-wrought interest. The weakest romance is not so stupefying as the lower forms of religious exciting literature, and the worst romance is not so corrupting as false history, false philosophy, or false political essays. But the best romance becomes dangerous, if, by its excitement, it renders the ordinary course of life uninteresting, and increases the morbid thirst for useless acquaintance with scenes in which we shall never be called to act. (82–83)

Despite this caution, however, he maintains in "Of Kings' Treasuries" that "the essence of all vulgarity lies in want of sensation" and that sensation is "the guide and sanctifier of reason itself" (45–46). Moreover, in embracing sensation, he asserts, the reader will become more adverse, not less, to the "monstrous" crimes depicted in sensation novels. As he says:

> In true inbred vulgarity, there is a dreadful callousness, which, in extremity, becomes capable of every sort of bestial habit and crime,

without fear, without pleasure, without horror, and without pity. It is in the blunt hand and the dead heart, in the diseased habit, in the hardened conscience, that men become vulgar; they are for ever vulgar, precisely in proportion as they are incapable of sympathy. (46)

As critics like Elizabeth Helsinger have noted, Ruskin exhorts his male readers to aim for a sensitivity to sensation that he represents as ideally feminine: "the 'tact' or 'touch-faculty' of body and soul: that tact which the Mimosa has in trees, which the pure woman has above all creatures; fineness and fullness of sensation, beyond reason" (46).

Ironically, however, this sensational sensitivity is achieved through rigorous critical analysis of the text, hermeneutic sophistication, and close reading. As the epigraph at the beginning of this section shows, Ruskin imagines that reading rightly involves doing violence to one's (vulgar) self that one may "clear the ground" for a newer better self.[12] In the opening of the lecture, Ruskin acknowledges that he is addressing an audience committed to education as it leads to "advancement in life" (28)—that is to say, his audience understands social position as contractual rather than fixed, and they imagine that education is a process of self-fashioning whereby one may effect an improvement in one's social position. Although Ruskin criticizes this kind of crass social climbing, he wholeheartedly endorses the idea that the right kind of reading counts as "an education which, in itself, *is* an advancement in Life" (28). And it is this education that demands a willingness to sacrifice the self through submission to the text. Ruskin provides his audience with a detailed example of how to do the right kind of close reading with a passage of Milton's "Lycidas." He describes the process "of the kind of word-by-word examination of your author" which requires:

watching every accent and expression, and putting ourselves always in the author's place, annihilating our own personality, and seeking to enter into his, so as to be able assuredly to say, "Thus Milton thought," not "Thus *I* thought, in mis-reading Milton." And by this process you will gradually come to attach less weight to your own "Thus I thought" at other times. You will begin to perceive that what *you* thought was a matter of no serious importance … in fact, that unless you are a very singular person, you cannot be said to have any "thoughts" at all; that you have no materials for them, in any serious matters;—no right to "think," but only to try to learn more of the facts. (43)

Here Ruskin berates his audience—they have "no right" to think or to claim the "I" of "I thought"—but he also encourages them to participate in the berating, to allow the text to teach them their worthlessness. In other words, what Ruskin theorizes is a contract between the reader and the text in which the reader agrees to acknowledge a stern master.

However, if Ruskin espouses hard discipline for his male readers in "Of Kings' Treasuries," he seems to exempt women from this self-immolating obedience in "Of Queens' Gardens." He advocates, in fact, that girls choose their own reading materials:

> She will find what is good for her; you cannot: for there is just this difference between the making of a girl's character and a boy's—you may chisel a boy into shape, as you would a rock, or hammer him into it, if he be of a better kind, as you would a piece of bronze. But you cannot hammer a girl into anything. She grows as a flower does. (83)

This would seem to suggest that girls, as organic beings, cannot be other than they are. They seem to have no access to the kind of contractual self-fashioning that Ruskin imagines in "Of Kings' Treasuries."

But for his girl readers too Ruskin envisions a profound affective relationship with texts, and it is this sensational sympathy that provides the route to masochistic reading for women. Ruskin urges that although Woman doesn't need scientific or factual knowledge,

> it is deeply necessary that she should be taught to enter with her whole personality into the history she reads ... to extend the limits of her sympathy with respect to that history which is for ever determined as the moments pass in which she draws her peaceful breath; and to the contemporary calamity, which, were it but rightly mourned by her, would recur no more hereafter. (81)

In entering into the suffering about which she reads, Woman should feel her own responsibility for it. As Ruskin claims, directly addressing his female readers: "There is no suffering, no injustice, no misery, in the earth, but the guilt of it lies with you" (90). Woman's masochism comes not through her powerlessness or passivity, but through an assumption of grandiose agency—a refined ability to recognize social injustices and an ownership of the guilt for *all* the misery caused by those injustices, which occur because women are not committed enough to heed or experience suffering. Thus, the degree of the woman reader's guilt is a measure of both her feminine virtue and her critical/perceptive faculties—the more guilt and shame she suffers in her reading, the more sensationally susceptible she shows herself to be, and thus the closer she comes to achieving Ruskin's queenly ideal. If Ruskin advocates formalist close reading for his men, he argues for politically-motivated cultural criticism for his women.

Critics rarely fail to remark on the difficulty of pinpointing Ruskin's position in Victorian culture—protean socialism against reactionary authoritarianism, reformist politics and aesthetics against social conservatism, doctrinaire gender ideology against "playfully" ambiguous prose.[13] In *Cultivating Victorians,* David Wayne Thomas argues evocatively that this difficulty stems in part from Ruskin's own vexed and contradictory attitudes toward individual agency and, moreover, that it is this very self-contradiction that makes Ruskin appeal to critics today, for whom "Ruskin's contradictions … can now be understood to reflect either his humanity or his heroic engagement with confusions and uncertainties that he has simply inherited from the culture at large" (80–81). While I find Thomas's account of Ruskin's contradictions persuasive, I would suggest that *Sesame and Lilies* paints a picture of Ruskin's understanding of ambivalent agency, rather than his ambivalent understanding of agency. In advocating a kind of willful powerlessness in relation to texts—sensational submission through close, critical analysis—Ruskin not only participates in his own culture's debates about productive power and critical detachment, but also acknowledges the disavowals to which twenty-first-century critics are liable. In other words, Ruskin's notion of sensational reading recognizes the critical reader's affective investments (and the sensational reader's critical awareness) in a way that criticism today often does not. And although Ruskin probably would not have admitted Collins's *No Name* and *Armadale* to the company of Milton and the "books of all time" (31), these novels promise their readers very similar kinds of suffering and similar rewards. They encourage the reader to cultivate an expansive, painful sympathy with transgression, which threatens the reader's comfort, even as it engenders his or her moral superiority.

NO NAME: "YOU DON'T KNOW WHAT I CAN SUFFER"

"You planned this marriage of your own free will," pursued the captain, with the furtive look and faltering voice of a man ill at ease. "It was your own idea—not mine. I won't have the responsibility laid on my shoulders—no! ... "

"Look at these," pursued Captain Wragge, holding up the envelopes. "If I turn these to the use for which they have been written, Mrs. Lecount's master will never receive Mrs. Lecount's letter. If I tear them up, he will know by tomorrow's post that you are the woman who visited him in Vauxhall Walk. Say the word! Shall I tear the envelopes up, or shall I put them back in my pocket?" ...

She raised her head; she lifted her hand and pointed steadily to the envelopes.

"Put them back," she said.

"Do you mean it?" he asked.

"I mean it."

—Wilkie Collins, *No Name* (1862)

No Name *possesses a simpler and more intense interest than* The Woman in White, *but it is a horrible and unnatural interest; the book enchains you, but you detest it while it enchains. The incidents ... are cleverly told, but the repulsiveness of the matter disturbs the pleasure of the reader.*

—Alexander Smith, Review of *No Name* (1863)

In this passage from Wilkie Collins's *No Name*, the swindler, Captain Wragge, questions the heroine Magdalen's resolve to go through with her marriage to her cousin (and foresworn enemy) Noel Vanstone. The letters that the captain holds out protect her false identity. They also stand as the visible symbol of Magdalen's conflicted desires. To order Captain Wragge to destroy the letters would be to release herself from the miserable prospect of using a disguise she hates to marry a man she hates. Yet the marriage to despicable, degenerate Noel Vanstone is the culmination of all of Magdalen's plotting and efforts; to marry him is to realize her desires. This conversation, like many others in the novel, underscores the fact that it is Magdalen's power to choose that determines the course of the plot (in both senses of the word). The question-and-answer format of the conversation enacts a verbal contract through which Magdalen reasserts her commitment to masochistic suffering.

This passage highlights precisely the reasons that *No Name* has been (and still is) problematic for sensation novel readers and critics.[14] First, the novel makes the reader privy to all the secret plotting and machinations, so that the tension of the plot cannot hinge on unrevealed secrets or hidden motives and actions. It demands, instead, that the reader's suspenseful pleasure come from experiencing, in minute detail, the execution of a clandestine plot. Second, the protagonist, Magdalen, is neither a heroically noble and pure suffering heroine nor a demonically conniving and evil villainess. Instead, the novel tries to present her as somewhere in between—a transgressive, guilty heroine, in constant and painful conflict with herself. *No Name* paradoxically demands a reader who is well disciplined and deviant—one who understands and accepts literary and social conventions, even as he or she is driven by the affective power of the novel to *feel* at odds with those conventions. Through its manipulation of the tropes of heroine (and villainess), plot, and sympathy, the novel forces the reader to examine individual agency in relation to the mechanisms of disciplinary power.

No Name presents a heroine who is an odd mixture of virtuous feminine ideal and "monstrous" perversion. In the beginning of the novel, for example, Magdalen is used as a foil to highlight the virtues of her elder and more-passive sister, Norah. When the parents' misdeeds and the daughters' plight are revealed, the narrator muses, through the governess, Miss Garth:

> Was the promise of the future shining with prophetic light through the surface-shadow of Norah's reserve; and darkening with prophetic gloom, under the surface-glitter of Magdalen's bright spirits? If the life of the elder sister was destined henceforth to be the ripening ground of the undeveloped Good that was in her—was the life of the younger doomed to be the battle-field of mortal conflict with the roused forces of Evil in herself? (147)

The answer, reiterated repeatedly throughout the novel, is a resounding yes. It is not just that Magdalen's actions are misinterpreted by others in the novel as bad;[15] she really does think and do evil things. Magdalen is punished for her parents' wrongs, one might say, but her subsequent plotting earns the punishment she has already unjustly received.[16]

But if Magdalen is not the ideal heroine—the helpless, virtuous victim of a Gothic plot, like Laura Fairlie in *The Woman in White*—neither is she a spectacularly demonized villainess like Lucy Audley in *Lady Audley's Secret*. Rather, she is an active agent in her own suffering. She conspires against her enemies, *and* she suffers acute moral pangs as a result. She transgresses, even as her "natural delicacy" revolts. She writes to her sister: "Try to forgive me. I have struggled against myself, till I am worn out in the effort. I am the wretched-est of living creatures ... If you knew what my thoughts are; if you knew how hard I have fought against them, and how horribly they have gone on haunting me in the lonely quiet of the house, you would pity and forgive me" (181). Magdalen's distress in contemplating her transgression and its attendant punishments is tempered with the imagined payoff for those transgressions. Her pleasure in transgressing comes from imagining having her actions judged by Norah. Notice, Magdalen imagines that Norah's knowledge of her (evil) thoughts would place Norah in a position to sympathize with rather than despise Magdalen. Likewise, the novel itself imagines a relationship with its reader in which intimate descriptions of the heroine's transgressions and suffering will place the reader in a similarly sympathetic position, despite the reader's knowledge/belief that Magdalen's behavior is wrong, that she is not "good."

In the preface to the 1862 edition of *No Name,* Collins describes his narrative strategy this way:

> It will be seen that the narrative related in these pages has been constructed on a plan, which differs from the plan followed in my last novel ... The only Secret contained in this book, is revealed midway in the first volume. From that point, all the main events of the story are purposely foreshadowed, before they take place—my present design being to rouse the reader's interest in following the train of circumstances by which these foreseen events are brought about. In trying this new ground, I am not turning my back in doubt on the ground which I have passed over already. My one object in following a new course, is to enlarge the range of my studies in the art of writing fiction, and to vary the form in which I make my appeal to the reader, as attractively as I can. (5–6)

It is clear here that Collins understands the problem with the "new ground" of *No Name:* the reversal of reader identification depends on making the transgression "attractive."

It is equally clear that critics both understood and rejected the project of reversing readers' sympathies. Margaret Oliphant, for instance, remarks in a review of *No Name* in *Blackwood's Magazine:*

> Mr. Wilkie Collins, after the skilful and startling complications of *The Woman in White* ... has chosen, by way of making his heroine piquant and interesting in his next attempt, to throw her into a career of vulgar

and aimless trickery and wickedness, with which it is impossible to have a shadow of sympathy, but from all the pollutions of which he intends us to believe that she emerges, at the cheap cost of a fever, as pure, as high-minded, and as spotless as the most dazzling white of heroines … This is a great mistake in art, as well as a falsehood to nature. ("Novels" 170)

Similarly, a reviewer for the *Reader* comments: "If Magdalen Vanstone could have sacrificed her character without sacrificing the sympathy of an ordinary English reader, it is impossible to say to what heights of sensational grandeur *No Name* might not have risen" (135). These reviews highlight the readers' difficulty with the novel: Magdalen is constructed by the text as a sympathetic heroine, but one cannot sympathize with her without also sympathizing with or condoning her "vulgar and aimless trickery and wickedness." If she were not sympathetic, then that trickery and wickedness would not create such a moral stumbling block; Magdalen would merely be a spectacular villainess. However, even if one were to view Magdalen antagonistically (a position not at all encouraged by the text), one's expectations would *still* be thwarted because Magdalen doesn't get punished for her wickedness. There is no comfortable reassertion of law and order at the end of the novel that leaves the villains properly contained (imprisoned in a mental institution, or executed by an agent of a secret Italian society, say) and "the good people all happy and at peace" (Braddon, *Lady Audley* 447).[17]

Despite the critics' insistence on the heroine's perversity, however, *No Name* shows that Magdalen's masochism is deeply imbedded in the rhetoric of ideal femininity. After the revelation of her parents' secret and her own lost fortune, Magdalen agrees with Mr. Clare to send Frank away for his own good:

> "You don't know me," she said firmly. "You don't know what I can suffer for Frank's sake. He shall never marry me, till I can be what my father said I should be—the making of his fortune. He shall take no burden when he takes me; I promise you that! I'll be the good angel of Frank's life." (167)

In order to be the Angel in the House, one must sacrifice oneself.[18] Indeed, this self-immolation in the name of romantic love (and domestic felicity) is practiced not only by Magdalen but also by her mother and her virtuous sister, Norah. As Norah says to her sister:

"The way to happiness is often very hard to find; harder, I almost think, for women than for men. But if we only try patiently, and try long enough, we reach it at last—in Heaven, if not on Earth" (311).

Similarly, the lawyer, in revealing the secret of the parents' transgression to Miss Garth, remarks of Mrs. Vanstone:

> Having once resolved to sacrifice her life to the man she loved; having quieted her conscience by persuading herself ... that she was "his wife in the sight of Heaven"; she set herself from the first to accomplish the one foremost purpose of so living with him, in the world's eye, and never to raise the suspicion that she was not his lawful wife. The women are few indeed, who cannot resolve firmly, scheme patiently, and act promptly, where the dearest interests of their lives are concerned. (130)

If all good women are masochists, this passage seems to imply, it is not because they are passive, but rather because they are tirelessly active plotters and secret-keepers. Given interests dear enough, women are capable of almost anything. This certainly is not an idea original to Collins. Indeed, the popular press was rife with stories of real women like Madeline Smith committing "crimes of passion." In 1842, conduct-book maven Sarah Stickney Ellis assured the "Daughters of England" that "to love, is woman's nature ... to be beloved, is her reward," even as she warned them that

> all women ... who have committed those frightful crimes which stain the page of history—all have acted from impulse, and by far the greater number have acted under the influence of misplaced affection. It is, indeed, appalling to contemplate the extent of ruin and of wretchedness to which woman may be carried by the force of her own impetuous and unregulated feelings. (15–16)

In other words, woman's virtue and woman's vice stem from the same thing, her innate "nature"—a nature, it should be noted, that is far from essentially passive, but rather overburdened with active passions and impulses.

The difference, then, between a good woman and a bad one lies in the regulation of that nature, in her sensitivity to her conscience and the censure of others, in her capacity to feel shame—in other words, in her susceptibility to internalized, interpellated discipline. In rhetoric very similar to Ruskin's version of Woman's guilt in "Of Queens'

Gardens," Henry Mayhew writes in *Criminal Prisons of London* (1862) of the difference between virtuous and criminal women:

> The most striking peculiarity of the women located in the London pris-
> ons is that of utter and imperturbable shamelessness. Those who are
> accustomed to the company of modest women, and have learnt at once
> to know and respect the extreme sensitiveness of the female character
> to praise or blame, as well as its acute dread of being detected in the
> slightest impropriety of conduct, or in the circumstances of the least
> unbecoming the sex, and have occasionally seen the blood leap in an
> instant into the cheeks, till the whole countenance has come to be suf-
> fused with a deep crimson flush of modest misgiving, and lighted up
> with all the glowing grace of innocence itself … can hardly comprehend
> how so violent a change as that which strikes us first of all in the brazen
> and callous things we see congregated within the female prisons, can
> possibly have been wrought in the feminine character. (465–66)

Here, ironically, shame and guilt become the markers not of mal-
feasance but of innocence. In this paradox of the innocent woman's
shame, the structure of the masochistic heroine becomes clear: she
feels the "acute dread of being detected" in any transgression, yet she
must—for whatever reasons are concurrent with the internal logic of
the text—act against her own pure impulses. Thus, the masochistic
heroine's plot depends upon her suspension between desiring to
achieve her ends and dreading the consequences of her means. The
suspense of *No Name* rests precisely on this circular logic, in which
the suffering of shame is both the mark of innocence and the impetus
for transgression, and transgression results in the suffering of intense
shame.

How then does the reader's identification with *No Name*'s active,
masochistic heroine work? What is the "law" set in effect by the act
of reading? Magdalen is not the murderous femme fatale we love to
hate, but a "lovable" heroine whose sins cause us pain, just as they
pain her, and whose punishment we both dread and expect, just
as she dreads and expects it. In the novel, the reader's suspense is
produced (and painfully sustained) by frozen scenes of anticipation,
like the one quoted earlier in this chapter, that contemplate the still-
imminent punishment that Magdalen (again and again) agrees to
bring upon herself. In one of her first uses of her power to suffer,
Magdalen insists, despite repeated pleas from her sister and her

friends not to, on seeing the letter from her uncle that gives the final refusal of the sisters' claim to any of the inheritance:

> "May I see it?"
>
> Mr. Pendril hesitated, and looked uneasily from Magdalen to Miss Garth, and from Miss Garth back to Magdalen.
>
> "Pray oblige me by not pressing your request," he said. "It is surely enough that you know the result of the instructions. Why should you agitate yourself to no purpose by reading them? They are expressed so cruelly; they show such abominable want of feeling, that I really cannot prevail upon myself to let you see them."
>
> "I am sensible of your kindness, Mr. Pendril, in wishing to spare me pain. But I can bear pain; I promise to distress nobody. Will you excuse me if I repeat my request?"
>
> She held out her hand—the soft, white, virgin hand that had touched nothing to soil it or harden it yet. (153)

This scene works on two levels—addressing both Magdalen's and the reader's masochism. Just as Magdalen reaffirms her commitment to read the letter, so too the reader must decide to continue reading and continue entering into Magdalen's pain.

The exchange between Pendril and Magdalen, like the one between Magdalen and Captain Wragge, enacts the ceremony of the verbal contract described by Henry Maine in *Ancient Law:* "Now, if we reflect for a moment, we shall see that this obligation to put the promise interrogatively ... by effectually breaking the tenor of the conversation, prevents the attention from wandering over a dangerous pledge" (273). For the reader this scene invokes the contract in that it highlights precisely the "dangerous pledge" we make if we agree to identify with Magdalen—that we will be forced to experience over and over her assertion of the *choice* to suffer—and it reaffirms that we are willing to identify with her anyway. The passage provides the reader with the pain/pleasure of an intensely suspenseful and overwrought scene in which Magdalen's will and capacity to suffer is showcased ("I can bear pain").

The danger to which Pendril draws Magdalen's attention (and which she accepts nonetheless) is that the letter is an object capable of polluting her "soft, white, virgin hand." Note, however, that Collins eschews rape imagery; the thing we see foremost is not penetration, but a grasping hand:

> Line by line … Magdalen read those atrocious sentences through,
> from beginning to end. The other persons assembled in the room, all
> eagerly looking at her together, saw the dress rising and falling faster
> and faster over her bosom—saw the hand in which she lightly held
> the manuscript at the outset, close unconsciously on the paper, and
> crush it, as she advanced nearer and nearer to the end. (155–56)

For Magdalen, reading her uncle's letter means laying claim to an
instrument of the law that exerts control over her and her sister, and
deriving satisfaction from the pain it produces.

The uncle's letter, in fact, becomes emblematic throughout the
novel of Magdalen's erotic pleasure in pain: she puts a copy of it,
along with a copy of her father's will and a lock of her lover's hair, in
a white silk purse which she carries in her bosom, taking it out at key
moments to reemphasize the emotional stakes of her plot. Clearly,
the law and sexual desire here become intermingled in Magdalen's
subjectivity. The purse stands unsubtly for enclosed and pure female
sexuality, yet the purse is already penetrated by the mechanisms of
the law (the will, the uncle's letter) and by the sexualized symbol of
her love for Frank (the lock of hair). Furthermore, the objects together
symbolize her own state of suspense: the will, perhaps, represents
her responsibility for her father's death,[19] or the inherited taint of
his bigamy; the letter represents the punishment she will incur by
scheming against her uncle; the lock of hair represents her ultimate
reward for having suffered. As Deleuze writes: "Formally speaking,
masochism is a state of waiting … The masochist waits for pleasure
as something that is bound to be late, and expected pain as the condi-
tion that will finally ensure (both physically and morally) the advent
of pleasure" (71).

It is interesting to note that Magdalen's pleasure and pain are
produced through her manipulation of the purse and its relics. In a
later scene we see how the suspension between her conflicting desires
(be a bad girl and win her money back, or be a good girl and quit
plotting against her cousin) is figured in the purse. She contemplates
her ability to use her sexuality to control Noel Vanstone in this
manner:

> "I can twist any man alive round my finger," she thought, with a
> smile of superb triumph … She shrank from following that thought
> to its end, with a sudden horror of herself: she drew back from the
> glass, shuddering, and put her hands over her face … Her eager

fingers snatched the little white silk bag from its hiding place in her bosom; her lips devoured it with silent kisses ... The tears gushed into her eyes. She passionately dried them, restored the bag to its place. (306)

"Triumph" in her power to do evil is transformed into horror and self-loathing, which is then immediately transformed into abject pleasure in sinning and suffering for Frank; Magdalen embraces with "eager fingers" and "devouring" lips her (to quote Mrs. Oliphant) "course of vulgar and aimless trickery and wickedness." It is this suspension between conflicting desires (pain and pleasure) that drives the plot of No Name.

Magdalen's plot to marry Noel Vanstone succeeds at the end of the fourth book, with the narrator's grim declaration: "It was done. The awful words which speak from earth to Heaven were pronounced. The children of the two dead brothers—inheritors of the implacable enmity which had parted their parents—were Man and Wife" (511). Arguably, this is the point at which the reader's relationship to the novel becomes most painful, and the effort to sustain the masochistic contract with the text most difficult. The remaining four books and three "Between the Scenes" interludes seem to eke out a bleak denouement in which Magdalen's fate is more and more thoroughly sealed. As Captain Wragge tells his wife: "She has gone her way ... Cry your cry out—I don't deny she's worth crying for" (513). Though Magdalen is still alive, the novel's "prophetic gloom" seems to have been realized. She has lost her purity, her chance to repent before it is too late, her connections to friends and family, which might have "saved her from herself." In the remaining chapters, Magdalen loses even the money for which she has sacrificed everything else when her husband writes her out of his will and then dies moments later. She gives up her position as a lady, and her last few hundred pounds, when she trades places with her servant to go in search of a Secret Trust that might allow her to contest the last-minute will. While searching for the Trust, she is caught and thus gives up any claim she had to the law's protection. Furthermore, throughout the course of her plotting, she has ruined her health, so that when she runs away from her employer's house with the police in pursuit, she succumbs to a life-threatening fever.

The reader's painful suspense here is no longer tied so much to the tension of Magdalen's conflicted desires and the increasingly faint chance of her redemption, as in the premarriage scenes. Now it depends instead on a familiarity with novelistic conventions and the inevitability of punishment equal to (or, as is more likely in Victorian fiction, exceeding) the crime. Fallen women, no matter how sympathetically rendered or how ultimately repentant, rarely come to good ends. (Lady Isabel Vane in *East Lynne*, Lady Dedlock in *Bleak House*, or Edith Dombey in *Dombey and Son* are just a few examples; without any trouble, one could think of ten more.) We might anticipate, therefore, a deathbed scene of confession and forgiveness with Norah, but not a happy ending for Magdalen. To continue reading after the marriage is merely to confirm what we already know and dread will happen. In this way, the reader is punished for his or her contractual agreement with the novel.

Of course, this isn't how *No Name* ends. In the last two chapters Magdalen gets all the good things that she is too wicked to deserve: the return to family and friends, her lost eighty thousand pounds, her health, and even the love of a man much superior to her original lover, Frank. What does this reward mean for the novel? One might be tempted to assume that it signifies some kind of rebirth on the heroine's part. This is the narrator's assertion: "So, she made the last sacrifice of the old perversity and the old pride. So, she entered on the new and nobler life" (737). Mrs. Oliphant didn't find this moral renaissance convincing, and given the final resolution of the novel, neither should we. Nor should we view the end of Magdalen's suffering as the end of her masochism. Rather than leaving behind her old perversity, Magdalen's new happiness depends on her reassertion of it.

Here again we see the significance of Magdalen's white silk purse. In Kirke we have an amalgamation of the dead father (for whom she mistakes Kirke in the delirium of her fever) and the object of desire, Frank. But we also have the third portion of her collection of fetishes. Kirke represents disciplinary authority as well—the threat of punishment. Before Magdalen can enter into the contractual relationship of marriage with Kirke, she must make another kind of contractual alliance with him: she must confess her sins and invite his judgment, as evidenced by her statement to him: "Oh don't encourage me in my own miserable weakness! Help me to tell the truth—*force* me to tell it, for my own sake if not for yours!" (728). Thus, the final reward for the heroine is realized only through the reiterated threat of disciplinary authority in the figure of Kirke rejecting her for her transgressions. That he does not reject her does not eliminate the threat of punishment. And, remember, it is the visibility of this punitive discipline that is crucial for the masochist's pleasure in the last scene:

> The next instant, she was folded in his arms, and was shedding delicious tears of joy, with her face hidden on his bosom.
>
> "Do I deserve my happiness?" she murmured, asking the one question at last. "Oh, I know how the poor narrow people who have never felt and never suffered, would answer me, if I asked them what I ask you. If *they* knew my story, they would forget all the provocation, and only remember the offence—they would fasten on my sin, and pass all my suffering by. But you are not one of them?" (740)

Here Magdalen has the last word on her subjectivity. She asks, "Do I deserve my happiness?" And she answers (implicitly), "Yes, because I have felt and suffered."

No Name demands, in the final scene as much as anywhere else in the novel, that the mechanisms of disciplinary power be visible; it is only through their visibility, after all, that one can linger over them and derive erotic pleasure from them, as the text invites the reader to do. In the final scene of the novel Magdalen's passionate tears in her moments of abject humiliation are converted to "delicious tears of joy." The masturbatory "silent kisses" with which she has formerly "devoured" her white silk purse are transformed into sexual union in the form of a verbal *and* nonverbal contract between her and Kirke:

> "Tell me the truth!" she repeated.
>
> "With my own lips?"
>
> "Yes!" she answered eagerly. "Say what you think of me, with your own lips."
>
> He stooped, and kissed her. (741)

We have been asked throughout to identify with Magdalen in her transgressions, to invest our desire in her secret-keeping. In the end, she is rewarded (as are we) not in spite of, but *because* of, those transgressions.

The moral of the story is not that disciplinary power doesn't work, but that it works very well indeed. Here the subject of the Panopticon, having internalized his or her position of "compulsory visibility," uses that position to perform "sinful actions" and to experience the erotic pleasure of the punishment attendant thereon. Furthermore, in eroticizing the disciplinary scene, masochism produces a "doubling-back" effect by which the "compulsory visibility" of the Panopticon is turned in on itself. Paradoxically, the novel makes tangible the successful machinations of disciplinary power—a power that, theoretically, is only effective insofar as it is intangible. *No Name* displays, through Magdalen, the production of a subject who is able, if not to escape, at least to examine and manipulate the machinery of her interpellation. Likewise, the novel allows the reader, through his or her identification with the masochistic heroine, to participate willingly in the process of his or her own subjection to the discipline of reading.

ARMADALE: "THE PAIN WHICH MIXES ITSELF WITH ALL PLEASURE"

"If we are to be parted again, it must be his doing or yours—not mine. The dog's master has whistled," said this strange man, with a momentary outburst of the hidden passion in him, and a sudden springing of angry tears in his wild brown eyes: "and it's hard, sir, to blame the dog, when the dog comes."
—Wilkie Collins, *Armadale* (1866)

Like *No Name, Armadale* imagines that agency is realized only when the subject "has lost all care" for itself. In *Armadale,* even more than in *No Name,* it becomes clear why the "oedipal logic" of masochism cannot be abandoned. In the novel, access to the father's name becomes synonymous with ownership of the father's sin, and the hero must struggle throughout the narrative to erase the grim inheritance attached to his name. The novel begins with the first (in order of appearance) of four Allan Armadales dictating his confession of murder as he lies paralyzed and dying from an undisclosed illness (presumably syphilis) contracted during a vicious life in Barbados, where he has finally married a mulatto woman and produced an heir, the second Allan Armadale, then an infant. He confesses that he inherited his name when the father of the original Allan Armadale (number three in order of appearance) disowned his son. Possessed of a new name and property in Barbados and England, Armadale prepares for an arranged marriage with an English heiress, only to find that the disinherited Armadale has swooped in and eloped with his betrothed (with the help of a scheming young servant girl, Lydia Gwilt, who will return later as the novel's murderous villainess), thereby securing for himself British lands and bride. In a fit of rage, the first Armadale murders his rival, but not before that rival has

impregnated his stolen bride, who later gives birth to Allan Armadale number four (who will, of course, later inherit those estates to
which his father aspired). Thus, a rivalry and a murder founded on
inherited British and colonial wealth and sexual jealousy constitute
the basis for all subsequent action in the novel. The words of the
dying father are as follows:

> "I, going down to my grave, with my crime unpunished and una-
> toned, see what no guiltless mind can discern ... I see the vices which
> have contaminated the father's name, descending, and disgracing
> the child's. I look in on myself—and I see My Crime, ripening again
> for the future ... and descending, in inherited contamination of Evil,
> from me to my son." (54–55)[20]

Donald E. Hall notes that for a novel that offers up the force of
patriarchal power in pursuit criminal femininity for its narrative
suspense, *Armadale* features a singularly inept set of manly detectives
and a singularly "desensationalized" villainess in Lydia Gwilt (166).
I would argue, however, that this is because most of the suspense
in *Armadale* resides not in the villainess's plotting, but in the heroes'
attempts to escape patriarchal power—in the murderer's son's vacillation between conflicting desires either to adhere to the father's
dying wish and assume hereditary responsibility for the crime, or to
repudiate the father by maintaining his alias, Ozias Midwinter, and
sacrificing himself to repay his debt of gratitude to the other junior
Allan Armadale, whom he calls his "master." Consider Midwinter's
conflicting drives: the command of the father to "be ungrateful, be
unforgiving; be all that is most repellant to your own gentler nature,
rather than live under the same roof, and breathe the same air with
[Allan Armadale]" (56), as opposed to the mandates of his own self-
immolating love and gratitude for Allan:

> "I do love him! It will come out of me—I can't keep it back. I love the
> very ground he treads on! I would give my life—yes, the life that is
> precious to me now, because his kindness has made it a happy one—I
> tell you I would give my life—." (122)

The novel describes this dilemma over and over as Midwinter's
"constant struggle": "Mercilessly in earnest, his superstition pointed
to him to go while the time was his own. Mercilessly in earnest, his
love for Allan held him back" (324).

Thus *Armadale* offers a version of "moral masochism," in which the morally superior, ethically sound position is the masochistic one. And this moral logic, in turn, demands that the novel itself reject the narrative structure of the bildungsroman, for if Midwinter attains his majority, he forfeits the redemption of his love for Allan. Midwinter's pleasure in his relationship with Allan, therefore, is always predicated on the pain of his self-annihilation. He is able to be Allan's friend only because he has abandoned his real identity and lived as a gypsy vagabond, but the social inferiority of his alias makes him "unfit" to be Allan's friend. For instance, when Allan has entrusted him with the stewardship of his estates, Midwinter says to Allan's mentor, Decimus Brock:

> "It is needless to tell you how I felt this new instance of Allan's kindness. The first pleasure of hearing from his own lips that I had deserved the strongest proof he could give of his confidence in me, was soon dashed by the pain which mixes itself with all pleasure—at least all that I have ever known. Never has my past life seemed so dreary to look back on as it seems now, when I feel how entirely it has unfitted me to take the place of all others that I should like to occupy in my friend's service." (188–89)

In fact, Midwinter, being smarter and more careful than Allan, is undoubtedly better suited to manage his affairs than Allan himself. Moreover, Allan's own irregular upbringing, alone with his mother (who was disowned by her family for her elopement with Allan's father) and without the benefits of a "gentleman's education," means that Midwinter's inferiority stems as much from his "sensitive self-tormenting nature" as it does from any real inequality (233).

The complex means by which the novel enlists our identification with this perverse hero depend, I would argue, on two things: first that Allan is not sympathetic, and second that Midwinter is. As the British Gentleman, Lord of the Manor, and manly subject upon whose meaty shoulders the inherited rights of property should naturally fall, Allan is too stupid, hearty, and psychologically shallow to offer the reader an "in." As the racially Other, the passionate and effeminate and mysterious social outcast, Midwinter presents psychological depth, via an extended first-person confession that offers the reader sympathetic purchase. Allan Armadale has no narrative space in the novel to explain himself or to tell his story to the reader: there are no instances of a sustained first-person narration by Allan, in letter or journal, with which Collins so often presents his protagonists' interiority. Instead Allan is always filtered through the perceptions of the narrator or the other characters, all of whom are more sensitive to the nuances of language than he. Conversely, Midwinter does have a first-person narrative, and he uses it precisely to avoid reproducing his father's sadism, to reinvent himself *through* his masochism, as a new man, without reference to his "father's influence."

In his confession (made to Mr. Brock to alleviate Brock's suspicions, so that Midwinter may be allowed to stay with Allan) Midwinter admits, first, to his hereditary guilt by allowing Mr. Brock to read the deathbed letter. This guilt is easily disposed of by Brock when he tells Midwinter: "I have no wish to treat you otherwise than justly and kindly ... Do me justice on my side, and believe that I am incapable of cruelly holding you responsible for your father's crime" (103). However, in the second half of his confession Midwinter recounts not his guilt, but his suffering. Furthermore, he differentiates between the suffering he has experienced unwillingly, helplessly (as a third party), under the sadistic logic of his father's inheritance, and the suffering he willingly accepts as part of a contract and as the means to escape his father's legacy. Because his mother and stepfather knew the secret of his father's crime, he has been subjected to punishment from his earliest memory, which he reveals to Brock:

> "[My parents] were both well aware that the shameful secret which they would fain have kept from every living creature, was a secret which would one day be revealed to *me* ... and there was I, an ill-conditioned brat, with my mother's Negro blood in my face, and my murdering father's passions in my heart ... I don't wonder at the horsewhip now, or the shabby clothes, or the bread and water in the lumber room. Natural penalties all of them, sir, which the child was beginning to pay already for the father's sin." (105–6)[21]

Yet we are clearly not meant to believe that he should be punished for his father's crime. Brock, hearing Midwinter's narrative, has already asserted that *he* won't blame Midwinter for his parents' sins. And the structure of the text—with Brock as stand-in for the reader, "hearing" the confession—invites the conclusion that we too should be incapable of that cruelty.

Even as we reject the injustice Midwinter has suffered from his parents, his schoolteacher and classmates, and the school watchdog who "left his mark" on Midwinter's body along with "his master's marks" (106), the confessional narrative carries us from the righteous indignation of Mr. Brock to the masochistic thrill of Midwinter's assuming the dog's role for himself. After leaving the school, Midwinter is "adopted" by a gypsy who, in his own words, gives Midwinter "'a new father, a new family, and a new name. I'll be your father; I'll let you have the dogs for your brothers; and if you promise to be very careful of it, I'll give you my own name into the bargain'" (107). Midwinter further explains that afterward

> "the dogs and I lived together, ate and drank, and slept together ... Many is the beating we three took together; many is the hard day's dancing we did together; many is the night we have slept together, and whimpered together, on the cold hillside. I'm not trying to distress you, sir; I'm only telling you the truth. The life with all its hardships was a life that fitted me, and the half-bred gipsy who gave me his name, ruffian as he was, was a ruffian I liked." (107)[22]

Brock's astonishment at Midwinter's affection for the "man who beat [him]" shows that he cannot enter into the masochistic economy in which Midwinter operates, but as Midwinter says to him: "Didn't I just tell you now, sir, that I have lived with the dogs? and did you ever hear of a dog who liked his master the worse for beating him?" (107). The difference between the beatings he receives from his stepfather and the schoolmaster and the ones he receives from his adopted father is, of course, that he *agrees* to the latter. He contracts with the gypsy to assume his new identity as one of his dogs. Perhaps we cannot appreciate the relationship between Midwinter and his cruel gypsy master, but by the time Midwinter has entered the "present" of the novel, he is not the gypsy's dog, but Allan's, and *that* relationship we are invited to endorse wholeheartedly. After all, as we have seen, it is this relationship that saves Midwinter—literally, in that Allan nurses him back to health when he suffers from a brain fever, and spiritually, in that it is his debt to Allan that allows him to rise above his father's sordid legacy:

> "Say if you like, that the inheritance of my father's heathen belief in Fate is one of the inheritances he has left to me. I won't dispute it; I won't deny that all through yesterday *his* superstition was *my* superstition. The night came before I could find my way to calmer and brighter thoughts. But I did find my way ... Do you know what helped me? ... My love for Allan Armadale." (120)

Thus, *Armadale* plays out Midwinter's life-and-death struggle to maintain his precarious, ecstatic/painful love-relationship with Allan and to guard against the "aggressive return" of his superstitions and his father's murderous legacy.

Ironically, that aggressive patriarchal return is embodied in the figure of the novel's villainess. The beautiful and deceitful Lydia Gwilt is the only surviving actor from the original conflict between the senior Armadales—the servant who forged letters to facilitate her mistress's elopement with the "wrong" (and soon-to-be murdered) Armadale. Lydia Gwilt figures as a threat not only to Allan and Midwinter's relationship but also to the stability of the narrative itself. Her introduction into the novel's world forces perverse allegiances to shift internally (among characters) and externally (between character and reader) when, midway through the third book and for the entirety of the fourth book, the reader's access to the plot comes almost exclusively through Lydia Gwilt's letters and diary. Through her diary we learn that she has discovered a way to inherit Allan's property in three easy steps: first, by marrying Midwinter (under his real name); second, by seeing to it that Allan dies conveniently far from home; and, third, by returning to Thorpe-Ambrose as Allan's widow (presumably with Midwinter also disposed of). This scheme is necessary to her very material well-being, as she herself states: "It is the salvation of me. A name that can't be assailed, a station that can't be assailed, to hide myself from my past life!" (540). Yet it fills her with horror because she has learned to love Midwinter and desire a "real" marriage with him. Thus we get simultaneous pictures of her as evil adventuress and suffering victim.

I would argue that both versions are temptingly sympathetic, although for different reasons. In her character as Allan's nemesis Lydia is not very nice, but she is witty and funny. Her descriptions of her prey are brutal, but they only repeat with added emphasis and irony what has already been said about Allan by the narrator and other characters. Here is her assessment of Allan: "He is a rattle-pated young fool—one of those noisy, rosy, light-haired, good-tempered men, whom I particularly detest" (343). Compare this to the narrator's slightly more indulgent introductory description: "His temperament, it could not be denied, was heedless to the last degree: he acted recklessly on his first impulses, and rushed blindfold at all his conclusions" (61–62). These are the very qualities—the "merciless gaiety of spirit" and the "ignorant self-possession and ... pitiless repose" (156)—that tempt even Midwinter (under the "noisome" influence of his father) to make Allan suffer by revealing his true identity.

Yet Lydia is also like Midwinter in her struggle to reject that sadism and to reinvent herself through her suffering. In her character as victim she exercises an appeal for the reader, like Midwinter's, based on her ability to confess her sins and articulate her suffering. The first-person narrative of her journal becomes, at least temporarily, less about her plotting against Allan and more about her being at war with herself, torn between her desire to plot against Allan and her desire to forfeit her schemes and to be punished and thereby redeemed. In some ways this articulation of her suffering and sins, and her desire for punishment/absolution, work exactly like Midwinter's confession to Brock—that is, they facilitate the reader's identification with a flawed or suspicious, but suffering, character. Yet unlike Midwinter's confession, or Magdalen's to Captain Kirke in *No Name*, Lydia's diary ultimately fails to authorize her redemption. She cannot rise from the ashes of her past, as Midwinter does, to become someone's grateful "dog," although she comes very close:

> I was within a hair's breadth of turning traitor to myself. I was on the very point of crying out to him, "Lies! all lies! I'm a fiend in human shape! Marry the wretchedest creature that prowls the streets, and you will marry a better woman than me!" … I wish I had been born an animal. My beauty might have been of some use to me then—it might have got me a good master. (594)

Lydia's bid for redemption fails for a number of reasons, most important of which is that for her to assume a masochistic position in the novel, she needs to contract an alliance with a master and protector—a role for which she fails to secure Midwinter's cooperation, though he does marry her. Midwinter's choices have already been laid out for him prior to his involvement with Lydia: choose the happiness of submission to Allan, or choose to relinquish that relationship by accepting his father's murderous legacy. Clearly, to accept the father's legacy is wrong according to the moral logic of the novel. Therefore, to accept mastery over Lydia is to remove himself from his morally superior role as masochist and to assume the role of sadist. As Lydia writes in her journal: "I could bear it if I loved him less dearly than I do. I could conquer the misery of our estrangement if he only showed the change in him as brutally as other men would show it. But this never has happened—never will happen. It is not in his nature to inflict suffering on others" (659).

The transformation that Lydia attempts—from sadistic mistress to submissive wife—fails, I would argue, precisely because Midwinter refuses to abandon *his* submissive relationship to Allan. This love triangle is expressed unequivocally in Lydia's journal: "What maddens me, is to see, as I do see plainly, that Midwinter finds in Armadale's company ... a refuge from *me*" (669). Lydia is forced by Midwinter's declining interest in being her master, by Allan's constitutionally annoying personality, by "chance" circumstances, to resume her position as villainess, and this in turn allows Midwinter to consolidate his position as masochist by sacrificing himself to save Allan.

In the final showdown at the sanitarium—to which Lydia has lured Allan that she might poison him in his sleep, and to which Midwinter fortuitously finds his way in time to interfere—we see a brief moment of Lydia's success; she has, it seems, finally forced Midwinter to be her "master":

> Mr. Bashwood stole panic-stricken to her side. "Go in there!" he whispered, trying to draw her towards the folding doors which led into the next room. "For God's sake be quick! He'll kill you!"
>
> She put the old man back with her hand. She looked at him with a sudden irradiation of her blank face. She answered him with lips that struggled slowly into a frightful smile.
>
> "Let him kill me," she said.
>
> As the words passed her lips, [Midwinter] sprang forward from the wall, with a cry that rang through the house. The frenzy of a maddened man flashed at her from his glassy eyes, and clutched at her in his threatening hands. He came on till he was within arm's length of her—and suddenly stood still. The black flush died out of his face in the instant when he stopped. His eyelids fell, his out-stretched hands wavered, and sank hopeless. He dropped, as the dead drop. He lay as the dead lie, in the arms of the wife who had denied him. (758)

Coitus interruptus. The masochistic scenario begins, and then falls through, because Midwinter falters in the instant of meting out punishment, the prospect of which has called an "irradiated" flush to Lydia's face. But she gets no satisfaction: Midwinter's whole body suffers from erectile dysfunction.

The climax of the novel reads like a French farce of masochists—with everyone running up and down stairs, in and out of bedrooms, falling all over themselves to make sacrifices, to suffer, and thereby to be redeemed. Midwinter, suspecting (after his wife's betrayal) some violence against Allan, switches bedrooms with him so that he can lie patiently and wait to intercept the violence: "The one safeguard in his friend's interests that Midwinter could set up, was the safeguard of changing the rooms—the one policy he could follow, come what might of it, was the policy of waiting for events" (798). And of course Midwinter's plan works; he *is* able to sacrifice himself for Allan. Lydia mistakenly poisons him, leaving Allan snoring in his usual state of "pitiless repose" in the other room. Then, when Lydia discovers her mistake, she is able, at last, to achieve her masochistic role. She rescues Midwinter from the poisoned air in his bedroom and then enters the fatal room herself so that Midwinter might find happiness without her: "She bent over him, and gave him her farewell kiss. 'Live, my angel, live!' she murmured tenderly, with her lips just touching his. 'All your life is before you—a happy life and an honoured life, if you are freed from *me!*'" (806).

With the brief disruption of heterosexual union dismissed, the novel allows its perverse hero, and with him its perverse readers, to reap the rewards of his masochistic suffering. *Armadale* ends with Allan and Midwinter together on the eve of Allan's wedding to his own superfluous (and mostly absent) bride.[23] This marriage may be imminent, but *we* don't see it; instead, we see an intimate, passionate exchange between the "dog" and his "master" that confirms their mutual commitment to one another:

> [Allan] began, in his bluntly straightforward way. "Let's say something now, Midwinter, about your [future]. You have promised me, I know, that if you take to Literature, it shan't part us, and that if you go on a sea voyage, you will remember when you come back that my house is your home. But this is the last chance we have of being together in our old way; and I own I should like to know—" His voice faltered, and his eyes moistened a little. He left the sentence unfinished.
>
> Midwinter took his hand and helped him, as he had often helped him to the words that he wanted, in bygone time.
>
> "You would like to know, Allan," he said, "that I shall not bring an aching heart with me to your wedding-day? If you will let me go back for a moment to the past, I think I can satisfy you … Out of the horror and the misery of that night you know of, has come the silencing of a doubt which once made my life miserable with

groundless anxiety about you and about myself. No clouds, raised by my superstition, will ever come between us again … Does this help to satisfy you that I, too, am standing hopefully on the brink of a new life, and that while we live, brother, your love and mine shall never be divided again?" (814–15)

This passage, though lengthy, is important because, like so many others in both *Armadale* and *No Name,* it depends for its force on the repetition of "dangerous pledges." Allan begins by making his demands: "Let's say something now … about your future." He reiterates the terms of their contract (that Midwinter won't let any outside interests separate them). And Midwinter responds that he "shall not bring an aching heart to [Allan's] wedding," that "no clouds … will ever come between [them] again," and that their "love … shall never be divided again." Thus, the conclusion returns to the in-process nature of the masochistic fantasy: the renewal of vows, the restaging of commitment to the contract.

In a sense, the disclaimer in the preface to *No Name,* that "the only Secret contained in this book, is revealed midway in the first volume" (5), might be addressed to critics who scrutinize Victorian culture for the sensational revelations of hidden power. In place of the "mystery" of discipline to be unraveled, *No Name* and *Armadale* offer treatises on discipline. They remind us that to pick up a novel and read is to consent to submit to its affective power and to collaborate in the production of our selves as disciplined subjects. Yet they also remind us that despite our submission to the novel, the discipline of novel-reading does not necessarily produce a "docile" reader. If Collins's novels explore the possibilities for perverse attachments to discipline, however, Anthony Trollope's fiction written and published during the same years as *No Name* and *Armadale* imagines the reader's submission as a complex negotiation between critique and disavowal whereby the reader's attachments to sensationalism enable the novel to do the work of producing belief, and encouraging investment, in the system of heterosexual exchange.

CHAPTER TWO

Realism Theorizes
Speculative Investments

Ladies and Gentlemen, you who have so long distinguished our firm by a liberal pa-
tronage, to you I now respectfully appeal, and in showing to you a new article I beg
to assure you with perfect confidence that there is nothing equal to it at the price at
present on the market. The supply on hand is immense, but as a sale of unprecedented
rapidity is anticipated, may I respectfully solicit your early orders? If not approved of
the article shall be changed.

 Ladies and gentlemen,
  We have the honour to subscribe ourselves,
   With every respect,
  Your most obedient humble servants,
   BROWN, JONES, and ROBINSON,
    Per GEORGE ROBINSON.

 —Anthony Trollope, *The Struggles of Brown, Jones, and Robinson* (1862)

Certain accomplished novelists have a habit of giving themselves away which must
often bring tears to the eyes of people who take their fiction seriously. I was lately
struck, in reading over many pages of Anthony Trollope, with his want of discretion
in this particular. In a digression, a parenthesis or an aside, he concedes to the reader
that he and this trusting friend are only "making believe." He admits that the events
he narrates have not really happened, and that he can give his narrative any turn
the reader may like best. Such a betrayal of a sacred office seems to me, I confess, a
terrible crime.

 —Henry James, "The Art of Fiction" (1884)

Anthony Trollope is a risky investment for sensational critics. Certainly Trollope's contemporaries were more likely to consider him
the cure for sensationalism than one stricken with the disease himself. Frances Cashel Hoey, praising Trollope's "homogeneous and

consistent pictures," writes in an 1872 review: "The public, who eagerly swallowed the sensation poison for a time simultaneously tasted his dainty dishes with uninjured powers of appreciation; and now that the purveyors of golden-haired bigamists and gilded-saloon rascality have fallen into oblivion ... the world knows where to turn for the faithful portraiture of the present which alone it loves to study" (400). Similarly, Alexander Shand writes in his 1877 essay "Mr. Anthony Trollope's Novels": "His talent is emphatically of the serviceable order, and wears wonderfully well. There must obviously be a good deal of the mechanical about his assiduous literary toils, since he has the habit of delivering a regular supply of his work with most methodical precision" (455). The "faithful portraiture," "serviceable" talent, and "dainty dishes" are, of course, compliments that cut both ways. Trollope's fiction is not dangerous, erratic, or poisonous—indeed, it is beneficial to its readers—but neither is it exactly "art."

Critics today have echoed these assessments of Trollope's literary production in the marketplace. Patrick Brantlinger writes in *The Reading Lesson:* "The equation between fiction and money, literary imagination and fiscal credit ... [is] simultaneously basic to [Trollope's] practice of narrative realism and a powerful source of [his] own resentment against that practice" (121). That is, in his attention to matters economical Trollope lays claim to faithful representation of the "real" (as opposed to the romantic, sentimental, or sensational), but at the same time he grapples uneasily with his own status as producer of commodities for the literary marketplace. With slightly more condescension, George Levine writes of Trollope in *The Realistic Imagination:* "The professional storyteller is at work. To be sure, there is nothing here that implies the pressure of great art. The tone is conciliatory in a way that James would have found unfortunate. There is no evidence of a struggle to find new ways to get stories told" (185).[1] In this version of realist fiction, the economic is both the marker of verisimilitude—the cure for pathological attachments to sensationalism—*and* the stigma of "vulgar" concerns, both for characters within the narrative and for the authors who "produce" the narratives for consumption.

Yet I contend that Trollope and his brand of realism have provided fertile ground for sensational critics, precisely (if paradoxically) because he is so unsensational. In a way, Henry James set the tone for Trollope criticism in 1884 when he revealed Trollope's "great crime": not only does Trollope's fiction not aspire to be "art," but it also refuses to let its readers forget that it is only a commodity, manufactured for their consumption and catering to their tastes. James deplores the narrative aside because it hampers his absorption by the text or, one might say, disrupts his unconsciousness of the artificiality of his attachments to the novel. He insists: "[Fiction] must take itself seriously for the public to take it so … The only reason for the existence of the novel is that it *does* compete with life" (288).[2] But James's characterization of Trollope's fiction works in two directions: if it shows Trollope's unwillingness to allow his readers to forget that they are consuming fiction, it also allows James to sensationalize his *own* narrative. Trollope is a tradesman, workmanlike and mechanical; James, on the other hand, is a detective, revealing a breach of a "sacred trust" and uncovering a "great crime." As I will argue in this chapter, this construction of Trollope's antisensational sensationalism has had two effects on contemporary criticism. First, it has enabled a "criticism marketplace" to prosper, wherein stories of the sensational commodity are sold and bought and, moreover, in which romances of the sensational realist critic abound. Second, it has elided the extent to which Trollope did, in fact, theorize his art outside the ubiquitous literary marketplace.

Trollope's *An Autobiography* has often been held up as a clue to his "criminally vulgar" attachments to writing as a profession. Indeed, as Frederic Harrison writes in 1895, the list of novels and the money earned for them, with which Trollope ends *An Autobiography*, must convince his readers that they have been swindled:

> When … he let the public into the story of his method, of his mechanical writing so many words per hour, of his beginning a new tale the day after he finished the last, of his having no particular plot, and all the little trade secrets of his factory, the public felt some disgust and was almost inclined to think it had been cheated out of its £70,000. (204)

Certainly one can read the passage from *The Struggles of Brown, Jones, and Robinson* with which I began this chapter in that light. In the preface to this fictional memoir, Trollope's narrator George Robinson appeals to his reading public, offering the memoir itself as the last item for sale by the bankrupt firm, thereby demanding that the novel be read as a commodity.

Yet if Trollope understood the market value of his fiction (what it was worth), he also understood its productive power (what it could do). For example, in his 1879 essay "Novel-Reading," Trollope writes of the role of Dickens's fiction:

> To whom has not kindness of heart been made beautiful by Tom Pinch, and hypocrisy odious by Pecksniff? The peculiar abominations of Pecksniff's daughters are made to be abominable to the least attentive reader. Unconsciously the girl-reader declares to herself that she will not at any rate be like that. This is the mode of teaching which is in truth serviceable. Let the mind be induced to sympathize warmly with that which is good and true, or be moved to hatred against that which is vile, and then an impression will have been made, certainly serviceable, and probably ineradicable. It may be admitted in regard to Dickens's young ladies that they lack nature … but they have affected us as personifications of tenderness and gentle feminine gifts. We have felt each character to contain, not a woman, but something which will help to make many women. (34–35)[3]

As Trollope suggests, the novel, if it is a commodity, contains more than its market value; it contains the "something" extra that through the emotional investments of "girl-reader[s]" will "help to make many women." Trollope's language of productivity doesn't quite make sense if we imagine the novel as only consumer goods. If, however, we consider the novel as operating in an economic register of speculation and investment, then the language of Trollope's essay adds up: a novel is not only a commodity—a "dainty [or poisonous] dish"—it is, also, an investment opportunity, offering rich dividends for the reader's investment.

Trollope thus posits what we might call, a bit ironically, a pre-Foucauldian Foucauldian theory of productive power. In articulating the novel's place in culture, he imagines his fiction as participating not just in the literary marketplace but in larger social discourses about marriage and economics. As such, his novels occupy an important if vexed position, producing (disciplining) subjects within a fluid social system. But even though Trollope claims that the "girl-reader" will be affected "unconsciously" by what she reads, his novels by no means suppose a willing or unconscious submission on the reader's part. Even as they encourage sensational investments in romance, the novels perversely test the strength of those attachments. The novels in this chapter all seem to come with the implicit caveat "If you will buy this, you will buy anything."

It is through this understanding of his narrative project that I consider three of Trollope's problem novels. First, I discuss two domestic novels: *Can You Forgive Her?*, the first in the Palliser series, and the less well-known *Miss Mackenzie*. In these Trollope's realism competes with itself: on the one hand, it seems to reject romance as untrue to life, but on the other hand, Trollope affirms the importance of the poetical and romantic stories—not because they are true but because they are *necessary* for the functioning of society. For instance, the narrator in *Miss Mackenzie* remarks: "I believe that a desire to get married is the natural state of a woman at the age of—say from twenty-five to thirty-five, and I think also that it is good for the world in general that it should be so" (136). Here the novel expresses not only belief in, but also the *need* for belief in, its own romance plot. To invest in a Trollope novel is to buy stock in "the love story." But to buy into the investment opportunity is to disavow the unpoetical, and even dangerous, social realities that the novels reveal. High risk equals high yield.

At the end of this chapter I will return to the "problem" of Trollope's very much underappreciated novel *The Struggles of Brown, Jones, and Robinson*, which even James Kincaid describes as "that deformed child only [Trollope] has ever loved" (*Novels* 164). *The Struggles* not only makes it impossible to buy into the myths of romance, but it theorizes the novel's role in the production of belief in those very myths. Although the novel is ostensibly a satire on trade, and as part of its satire represents novels as salable commodities, it does so, I argue, only to undermine the reader's faith in the existence of those same "vulgar" things with which it was so concerned. In *The Struggles* Trollope considers the author of realist narrative not as a producer of commodities, one who caters to the tastes of his buyers, but as a producer of belief, one who creates his readers' investments in the "real." To understand how Trollope's realist novels might work as investment opportunities, however, I will first consider present-day sensational investments in realism and then turn to a discussion of Victorian speculative investments, both financial and literary.

THE SENSATIONAL COMMODITY

The commodity in Victorian culture is as good as a fingerprint in wet paint to the forensic investigator, building a sensational story out of real things. As a theoretical framework for literary analysis, it has paid rich dividends to Victorian scholars, offering a vocabulary at once reassuringly materialistic—grounded in Marx's own theory of *Capital*, a language of *things*—and tantalizingly symbolic, evocative of appetites, desires, needs, and wants. Christoph Lindner writes in his 2003 *Fictions of Commodity Culture:* "The commodity figures throughout the fiction of the nineteenth and twentieth centuries as a living object of consumer fetish that excites desire yet strangely denies satisfaction" (3).[4] Certainly part of the desire elicited by the commodity is the desire of critics to delineate its form and function in culture. Indeed, in her 1999 essay "Production, Reproduction, and Pleasure in Victorian Aesthetics and Economics," Regina Gagnier describes the shift in critical attention from production/reproduction to commodity culture in recent decades as "the feminist, gay, and multicultural … defense of desire, especially the desire of the forgotten peoples of modernity for the goods and services of the world (including sexual goods and services)" (128). Thus, the commodity has assumed subversive weight in critical discourse. Critical accounts of the novel-as-commodity, however, have often emphasized the regulatory effects of consumer culture. Laurie Langbauer sums up this outlook in *Novels of Everyday Life* (1999): "The serial [novel]'s most important ideological work was to produce and determine an audience for itself" (9). Consequently, the Victorian realist-novel-as-commodity has operated as a tool of both disciplinary power (for the Victorians) and political resistance (for Victorianists).

Attention to the economic in Victorian literature and culture becomes a brand of "realist" criticism, as opposed to the ahistorical (and therefore "romantic") criticism offered by, for example, psychoanalysis or deconstruction. Yet in uncovering the Victorians' preoccupation with "vulgar" commerce, critics offer sensational secrets to their readers. In other words, through its paradoxically privileged and stigmatized position in Victorian culture, the economic offers for scholars both the mark of verisimilitude and the sensationally dirty secret of realist fiction. For example, Elsie Michie, in "Buying Brains: Trollope, Oliphant, and Vulgar Victorian Commerce" (2001), claims on the one hand that the novels in her study (*The Last Chronicle of Barsetshire* and *Phoebe Junior*) "function in a quasi-anthropological sense, evoking, through the drama of individual characters' financial problems, an entire culture's response to dramatic changes in economic practices and theory taking place in the last third of the nineteenth century" (78). And, on the other hand, she describes this cultural response to the economic, as represented by the novels' characters, as "the peculiar amalgam of pain, shame, and pleasure [they] feel as they become implicated in the credit economy" (78). Hence, Michie produces both a scientific (anthropological) account of Victorian commercial culture and, simultaneously, a sensational account of the "seductions of the material world" (79) hidden within the prosaic fiction of those least sensational of authors, Trollope and Oliphant.

More recently, some critics have shifted attention away from the consideration of novels as commodities to the analysis of texts (fictional and otherwise) participating in the production of meaning within the Victorian financial system. Thus, the 2002 special issue of *Victorian Studies* on "Victorian Investments" presented essays focusing on "the quotidian experiences of Victorian investors—what they read, wrote, knew, and felt about their investments and about the transformations of language, literary form, corporate organization, and political legislation within their culture that accompanied transformations in investment practices" (Schmitt et al. 7).[5] In paying attention to investment practices, these essays reveal the extent to which Victorian accounts of economic practices and relationships must be understood as participating in a symbolic economy as well as a material one.[6]

Most evocatively, "Writing About Finance in Victorian England," Mary Poovey's essay in the aforementioned *Victorian Studies* special issue, offers a theoretical framework through which to view the "exchanges and crossovers at the level of themes and formal features that drew financial journalism and realist novels into a relationship of generic proximity" (19). For Poovey both literary realism and financial writing are about exploring the question of how the value of the subject is constituted in the constructions "'What I am' and 'What I am worth'" (32).[7] Poovey's analysis offers a very useful complication of the pervasive metaphor of the "literary marketplace" by showing how both financial journalism and literary realism are concerned with telling stories to their publics, the value of which depends on their believability, but the generic functioning of which, conversely, depends on their "secrecy," or at least on their selective disclosure.

But, like commodity-centered analyses, Poovey's account constructs the financial as the sensational secret of realist fiction. Her view of the incorporation of "economic entanglements as determining factors in the novel's action" in *The Mill on the Floss* is this: "[Eliot] explores the emotional response that many contemporaries must have had to that half-visible, half-hidden financial system that was simultaneously inescapable and elusive" (36). Consequently, the financial system becomes Victorian Britain's unconscious—constitutive of quotidian experience, yet beyond conscious cognition. Naturally enough, therefore, the twenty-first-century critic's task is like the psychoanalyst's—uncovering the hidden truth of the Victorians' investments. Poovey demonstrates this in the final lines of the introduction to her anthology of Victorian financial texts:

> With the advantage of hindsight, we can know more about the nineteenth-century financial system than most of its participants could, but much valuable information is still lost to us forever because records were imperfectly collected and the desire for secrecy or drama too often influenced those who wrote about the system. This unavoidable mix of clarity and obscurity ... makes representations of the financial system all the more intriguing, for it encourages us to read selections like the ones collected here as generically ambiguous—as gestures toward accuracy that nevertheless draw many of their most effective conventions from some of the literary forms that flourished in the nineteenth-century: melodrama, romance, the detective story, and sensationalism. (*The Financial System* 33)

This conclusion to Poovey's introductory essay operates as a sensational twist ending. The "real" of financial writing has become the romantic, the mysterious, and the melodramatic.[8] Not only does she describe explicitly the Victorians' desire for secrecy and drama, but she also implicitly encourages a similarly sensational desire in *her* readers to see secrets revealed.

Poovey's language here—which casts the Victorianist scholar as the skeptical reader uncovering the hidden desires (for secrecy and drama) of financial authors—is reminiscent of Freud's language in discussing the analyst's role in uncovering the causes of hysteria. As Freud advises the analyst:

> Imagine that an explorer arrives in a little-known region where his interest is roused by an expanse of ruins ... He may content himself with inspecting what lies exposed to view, with questioning the inhabitants—perhaps semi-barbaric people who live in the vicinity,

about what tradition tells them of the history and meaning of these archaeological remains … But he may act differently. He may have brought picks, shovels, and spades with him, and he may set the inhabitants to work with these implements. Together with them he may start upon the ruins, clear away the rubbish, and, beginning with the visible remains, uncover what is buried. ("Aetiology" 97–98)

For Freud the work of the analyst is the archaeological excavation of repressed experience of which the patient is unaware, whereas for Poovey the Victorianist is privileged to see the "mix of clarity and obscurity" that would itself have been hidden from the Victorians themselves. Both passages rely on two mutually enforcing binary oppositions: The first establishes the "subject" (the Victorian participant in the financial system or the psychoanalytic "patient") as possessed of a split consciousness, with some fundamental information not available for conscious review. The second places the researcher/analyst in possession of the "hindsight," which can penetrate the obscurities of that split subject and, as a result, "know more."[9]

Yet, as I will show in the next section, although the Victorians certainly did sensationalize the economic realm, they also understood well their own desires for mystery and romance in that realm. Indeed, it was precisely this sensationalizing of money matters that enabled the financial system to operate.

SPECULATIVE INVESTMENTS IN THE STOCK MARKET AND IN THE ROMANCE

The parable of the talent in the napkin applies as forcibly to commercial and financial Europe in the nineteenth century as to agricultural Syria in the beginning of the first. The rayah of Hindustan who builds his rupees into the mud walls of his hovel, the French peasant who invests his five-franc pieces in the thatch of his cottage or among the roots of his cabbage-beds, may live on rice or maize, as the case may be, and go jogging along from the cradle to the grave as mildly useful members of society. But what would become of the movement of the world if everybody were to imitate their passive prudence?
—Alexander I. Shand, "Speculative Investments" (1876)

If I were to make my way into the house of any one of you as a chance visitor, and begin to teach your sons and daughters how to make love and how to receive love-making, you would think me to be a very dangerous and impertinent fellow … But when I, or some greater professor, come on the same errand with Mr. Mudie's ticket

on my back, you admit me, and accept my teaching … Would the love-making of our
world be done better without the teaching of such professors? That it should be done
is an essential necessity of our existence. That it should be done well, perhaps, of all
matters in our own private life the most important to us.

—Anthony Trollope, "On English Prose Fiction
   as a Rational Amusement" (1870)

It is not surprising that the economic realm was sensationalized by Victorians and in Victorian realism, for as the British economic system came more and more to depend on the stock market, and more and more individuals invested their personal capital in the system, the rise and fall of the market came increasingly to seem tied to individual interests.[10] Moreover, the precipitous rise in the number of joint stock companies brought about a similarly spectacular rise in the circulation of advertisements and articles touting investment opportunities and cautioning against reckless speculation.[11] In his attack on the system of selling the national debt, "The National Debt and the Stock Exchange" (1849), W. E. Aytoun tells a story that sounds very much like a sensation novel or melodrama. He describes speculation in the national debt as "the spirit of public gambling, which … has manifested itself periodically in this country—the fever-fits which seem to possess the middle classes of the community, and, by conjuring up visions of unbounded and unbased wealth, without the necessary preliminary of labour, to extinguish their wonted prudence." Moreover, he says of the "eldest offspring" of the national debt, the Stock Exchange:

> Marvellous indeed are the scenes to which we are introduced, whether we read its history as in the time of William of Orange, enter it at the period when the South Sea bubble had reached its utmost width of distension, or tread its precincts at a more recent date, when railway speculation was at its height … No stranger, indeed, may enter the secret place where its prime mysteries are enacted. (668)

In this system, which "has been pregnant with social and moral evils which have extended to the whole community" and in which "all sorts of deep-laid schemes [are] hatched" (667–68), everyday middle-class folks have been afflicted with secret crimes and insanity, the dangerous progeny of dissolute parents have come home to wreak havoc, and it is the author's job to reveal those lurid mysteries.

Indeed, Aytoun begins his essay by assuring his readers of the sensational qualities of the stock exchange: "We dare say, that no inconsiderable portion of those who derive their literary nutriment from Maga, may be at a loss to understand what element of romance can lie in the history of the Stock Exchange" (655). The "romance" of the stock exchange rests with the public who invest stories of lucrative financial opportunities with personal desires and attachments, but it also rests with a different public who, at a remove from the "infuriated and infatuated gambling" (670), read the exposé accounts of the market from authors like Aytoun.

Alexander Shand, in his 1876 essay "Speculative Investments," theorizes the necessity of sensationalism in the financial world, although, like Aytoun, he begins by bemoaning the dangerous "fever" that it produces:

> So the fever flame of an agitation in Egyptians or Peruvians is always being fanned by fresh announcements, each of them apparently authenticated by pieces of circumstantial evidence. Half-a-dozen times in a day, a bellow and roar in the Stock Exchange may greet the arrival of some new sensation, to be followed by a rush of sales or purchases; and the property that is liable to be blown about with each breath, naturally comes to be more doubtfully regarded. (196)

According to Shand, the appetite for rumors, scandals, and agitating stories of hot new investment opportunities amounts to a weakness for sensational narrative. As he says: "What seems to us more serious [than corruption] as a habitual danger, is the increasing tendency to sensational writing" (196). Thus, as Poovey suggests, the economic realm underwent no imaginative transformation to *become* sensationalized within the plots of novels. Rather, the melodramatic highs and lows, the sinister mysteries and lightning reversals of fortune, were already fully imagined within economic discourse.

However, the reliance of the stock market on selling "on spec" meant that the circulation of economic capital depended on the ability of stock companies to accrue symbolic capital. As the establishment of the spurious joint stock company, the South Central and Mexican Railway, in Trollope's *The Way We Live Now* shows, money is not necessarily made in the building of a real railroad, but in presenting the appearance of a legitimate corporation that *might* build a railroad. In other words, the investment economy cannot function without investors who are willing to "buy" what the companies are selling. This means, essentially, that stock frauds, scandals, and bubbles aside, the system must have investors to function; therefore, the sensational appeal is not to be disparaged. As Shand's retelling of the parable of the talent in the napkin illustrates, prudence carries its own risks.

Shand creates his own parable to illustrate for his readers the dangers of "passive prudence": a widow left with £5,000 has the choice of protecting her little bit of capital by investing conservatively and eking out an existence for herself and her "growing family" on the modest yearly interest, or of having "recourse to some of those more highly-priced stocks which are the refuge of the widow, the clergy-man, and the reckless" (175). In the first case,

> she finds that with her £150 to £220 [yearly interest], she is not only embarrassed as to providing food, clothing and houseroom for her growing family, but that she is compromising their future beyond remedy, from better fortunes. She is falling out of the circle of family acquaintances where her boys would be likely to find helpful friends and her girls to make happy marriages.

But, in the second case, "the clouds that hang over the future begin to dissipate, as the shadows are lifted from her everyday life" (175). Shand's explicit linking of the widow's investment of her of £5,000 to the "happy marriages" of her daughters in the future suggests that the persuasive appeal of the romance plot is one that informs the economic realm as much as economics infiltrates the plots of realist novels. His illustration also highlights the problem of female agency within both the economic and the emotional realm.[12] The widow is both the steward of her children's futures and an agent in the financial realm. In a sense, her emotional investments in happy endings for her children inform her financial investments in risky stocks. She must believe in the happy endings, despite her knowledge of the dangers, or to put it another way, she must forget what she knows of the dangers so that she may invest. Shand's article places his readers in a similar position of knowledge and disavowal in regard to the "seductive lottery of the Stock Exchange" (176), cognizant of the perilous realities of speculative investments, which he describes in detail, but assured nonetheless that "people must invest" (177).

It is this imperative—people must invest—that Trollope ponders in his fiction and criticism. The productive work that Trollope undertakes, however, is by no means a straightforward sell. Rather, he imagines a skeptical audience, reading decidedly unromantic fiction. In "On English Prose Fiction as a Rational Amusement," he reassures his audience that readers are not too susceptible to the dangerous influences of fiction:

> As to that pernicious way of looking at the affairs of life which is attributed to novel-reading,—that Lydia Languish determination, for instance, not to be married without the aid of a rope ladder,—I do not think that such result comes from the novels of our period … The manner of looking at life engendered by the novels of the day is realistic, practical, and, though upon the whole serviceable, upon the whole also unpoetical, rather than romantic. (112)

The problem, rather, as Trollope sees it, is that readers may not be susceptible enough. "The love-making of our world," we have already seen him state, "is an essential necessity of our existence" (109). What happens, then, if people refuse to participate? What if people are not attached to romance? Or what if something else is more attractive? These are the questions that Trollope asks in *Can You Forgive Her?* and *Miss Mackenzie.* The answer: then the task of "professors" like Trollope—to teach the "love-making of the world"—is that much more imperative and that much more vexed.

In *An Autobiography,* Trollope comments on *Miss Mackenzie:*

> [It] was written with a desire to prove that a novel may be produced without any love; but even in this attempt it breaks down before the conclusion. In order that I might be strong in my purpose, I took for my heroine a very unattractive old maid, who was overwhelmed with money troubles; but even she was in love before the end of the book, and made a romantic marriage with an old man. (172)

As critics have noted, Trollope's insistence on comic resolution is a position that is constantly assaulted from within his own writing.[13] But we might read his account of the novel's inexorable drift into romance, as if against his will, as a kind of advertising copy—establishing credit in the inevitability of romance. As the character George Robinson says, in *The Struggles of Brown, Jones, and Robinson,* "Get credit, and capital will follow" (4). Like George, both *Can You Forgive Her?* and *Miss Mackenzie* undertake to "sell" belief in romance to readers increasingly skeptical of its charms and its necessity, so that the "real thing" might follow.

As I have discussed previously, the "Woman Question" debates at the midcentury were highlighting both woman's victimization under the current marriage laws and the lack of any alternative for most women. But as Alexander Shand's "Speculative Investments" shows, the stock market provided single women appealing, if dangerous, opportunities for exercising their agency and achieving financial independence. If in speculative investments a woman risked losing all her capital, in marriage she was sure to. Frances Power Cobbe famously illustrates in her 1868 essay "Criminals, Idiots, Women, and Minors" that married women were the same under the law as convicted murderers, children, and the mentally incompetent. She begins the essay with the parable of the alien visitor who comes to England and observes a marriage: "Pardon me; I must seem so stupid! Why is the property of the woman who commits Murder and the property of the woman who commits Matrimony, dealt with alike by your law?" (109). Activists like Cobbe, Barbara Leigh Smith Bodichon, and Caroline Norton argued (and in Norton's case illustrated) that marriage was a risky speculation. The debates surrounding the Divorce and Matrimonial Causes Act of 1857, and Caroline Norton's highly publicized custody and divorce cases that preceded it, kept the "not-so-happily-ever-after" of marriage in the public eye in the 1850s and 1860s.[14]

Even further, these public discussions of the Act raised the question of whether it would not be better for a woman to remain single and self-sufficient than to be forced by financial exigencies into marriage. Cobbe observes in "What Shall We Do with Our Old Maids?":

> If, then, we seek to promote the happiness and virtue of the community, our efforts must be directed to encouraging *only* marriages which are the sort to produce them—namely, marriages founded on love … Where now, have we reached? Is it not to the conclusion that to make it a woman's *interest* to marry, to force her, by barring out every means of self-support and all fairly remunerative labour, to look to marriage as her sole chance of competency, is precisely to drive her into one of those sinful and unhappy marriages [of convenience]? It is quite clear we can never drive her into *love*. That is a sentiment which poverty, friendlessness, and helplessness can by no means call out. (87)[15]

Cobbe's argument cleverly makes financial independence the prerequisite for romance; while seemingly a contradiction, only by being independent will women be able to give themselves up to romantic alliances.

But if Cobbe claims that a woman cannot be made to love a husband because he saves her from "poverty, friendlessness, and help-lessness," Trollope's novels appear to respond to Cobbe's challenge. In fact, if we are to believe Trollope's dictums in "Novel-Reading" that "unconsciously the girl-reader declares to herself that she will not at any rate be like [Pecksniff's daughters]" and that "this is the mode of teaching which is in truth serviceable" (35), then Woman can indeed be "driven into love" if she can be persuaded to sympathize with the romances that she reads. To be sure, the "driving into love" is precisely the plot of both *Can You Forgive Her?* and *Miss Mackenzie.*[16]

In both novels the tension that Trollope describes as operating in *Miss Mackenzie*—romantic "in spite of" money troubles—is complicated ultimately not because the money troubles are subsumed by the dictates of romance at the novel's conclusion, but because the money itself is romantic, in two competing ways. First, the trouble with money is that it confers a freedom on women that blocks their easy entrance into the system of sexual exchange. To marry a woman with money is certainly a good thing, as the *Phineas* novels make clear, but a woman with money may find the romance of marriage less compelling. As Miss Todd, the "confirmed spinster," explains in *Miss Mackenzie:* "Now for me, I'm so fond of my own money and my own independence, that I've never had a fancy that way—not since I was a girl" (174).[17] And, indeed, although Miss Mackenzie does find the romance plot compelling, she is also envious of Miss Todd's independence. The narrator reminds us: "Miss Mackenzie, who was at present desirous of marrying a very strict evangelical clergyman, thought with envy of the social advantages and pleasant iniquities of her wicked neighbour" (174). But, second, money troubles make single life harrowing, frightening, and desolate. Counter to Cobbe's claim that love cannot be fostered by "poverty, friendlessness, and helplessness," in *Can You Forgive Her?* and *Miss Mackenzie* the heroines' financial dealings jeopardize their safety, thereby authorizing their rescue and reinvestment in romantic marriage resolutions. Given these intertwined investments (financial and romantic), the reader must, like the heroines, either be "rescued" and reclaimed by the domestic plot or, should she resist the novel's resolution, forfeit the payoff for her investment in the narrative.

CAN YOU FORGIVE HER?: "OF COURSE SHE HAD NO CHOICE BUT TO YIELD"

Of Can You Forgive Her? *I cannot speak with too great affection, though I do not know that of itself it did very much to increase my reputation. As regards the story, it was formed chiefly on that of the play which my friend Mr. Bartley had rejected long since ... The play had been called* The Noble Jilt; *but I was afraid of the name for a novel, lest the critics might throw a doubt on the nobility. There was more of tentative humility in that which I at last adopted. The character of the girl is carried through with considerable strength, but is not attractive.*

    —Anthony Trollope, *An Autobiography* (1883)

Mr. Bartley's earlier rejection of *The Noble Jilt* had, in fact, been based on how unattractive he found the heroine. In *An Autobiography* Trollope quotes his friend's letter, which he describes as "a blow in the face":

"As to the character of your heroine," [Bartley writes], "I felt at a loss how to describe it, but you have done it for me in the last speech of Madame Brudo." ... "'Margaret, my child, never play the jilt again; 'tis a most unbecoming character. Play it with what skill you will, it meets but little sympathy.' And this, be assured, would be its effect upon an audience. So that I must reluctantly add that, had I been still a manager, *The Noble Jilt* is not a play I could have recommended for production." (78–79)

The story fails, according to Mr. Bartley, because the audience can't sympathize with the "unbecoming character" of the heroine. This position is echoed by reviewers of *Can You Forgive Her?*. Henry James, for instance, offers a grumpy question and answer in his review in *The Nation:* "Can we forgive Miss Vavasor? Of course we can, and forget her, too, for that matter" (249). Similarly the critic in the *Spectator* opens his or her review with "Can we forgive her? asks Mr. Trollope. Certainly, if it were worth while, but we scarcely care enough about her for either a forgiving or unforgiving spirit" (247).[18] Thus, Alice Vavasor seems to oppose Trollope's claim that fiction "works" only inasmuch as "the mind be induced to sympathize warmly with that which is good and true, or be moved to hatred against that which is vile, and then an impression will have been made, certainly serviceable, and probably ineradicable"

("Novel-Reading" 34–35). Yet even if the reader does sympathize with Alice, then the novel presents other problems.

To wit, Alice Vavasor is perverse. At the opening of the novel she is twenty-four years old and has been in command of her own fortune since she turned twenty-one (7–8, vol. 1, chap.1). And she is engaged to marry a man whose main fault seems to be that he is "too perfect" (24, vol. 1, chap. 3). She rejects her excellent fiancé and attaches herself instead to a man she doesn't love, because "she had gone on thinking of it till she had filled herself with a cloud of doubts which even the sunshine of love was unable to drive from her heavens … [S]he had gone on thinking of the matter till her mind had become filled with some undefined idea of the importance to her of her own life" (109–10, vol. 1, chap. 11). And, of course, she violently regrets the decision once it is made: "She had done very wrong. She knew that she had done wrong. She knew that she had sinned with that sin that specially disgraces a woman … She understood it now, and knew that she could not forgive herself" (383–84, vol. 1, chap. 37). But even when she is rescued from her folly and restored to her worthy lover's arms, she seems in part to regret her happiness too: "Alice was happy, very happy; but she was still disposed to regard … her happiness as an enforced necessity" (361, vol. 2, chap. 75). Alice's vacillations refuse the novel's resolution even to the very end, suggesting that if the reader *were* to find her attractive rather than perverse, she would likewise have to feel ambivalently about the satisfactions offered by the "enforced necessity" of the happy ending.

However, Alice's perversity also has a strong narrative logic to it. Her desire to do something with her life manifests in ambitions that are both political and romantically novelistic:

> She would have liked, I think, to have been the wife of a leader of a Radical opposition, in the time when such men were put into prison, and to have kept up for him his seditious correspondence while he lay in the Tower. She would have carried the answers to him inside her stays,—and have made long journeys down into northern parts without any money, if the cause required it. She would have liked to have around her ardent spirits, male or female, who would have talked of 'the cause,' and have kept alive in her some flame of political fire. As it was she had no cause. (111, vol. 1, chap. 11)

Alice's ambitions and their source are interesting: in her desire to tramp around the country with no money, she sounds very much like she has been influenced by the example of Sir Walter Scott's heroine Jeanie Deans. Trollope, however, in "On English Prose Fiction," assures readers that Scott can exercise no dangerous influence on readers: "But no woman became forward, and no man a villain under [Scott's] teaching. Nor has he helped to produce domestic tragedies. No wife has left husband or child, stirred to mischief and vagabond propensities,—to what we, in the cant of the day, call Bohemianism,—through his influence" (115). Of course, Alice has been stirred precisely to those vagabond propensities that Trollope discounts.

John Grey is adamantly opposed to a career in politics, and so he will not offer Alice a "cause" in which to invest her energies. And although she loves him—indeed *because* she loves him—he represents a frightening loss of autonomy. As the narrator says of the political question:

> He had never argued … with her. He had never asked her to argue with him. He had not condescended so far as that. Had he done so, she thought that she would have brought herself to think as he thought … But she could not become unambitious, tranquil, fond of retirement, and philosophic, without an argument on the matter,—without being allowed even the poor grace of owning herself to be convinced. If a man takes a dog with him from the country up to town, the dog must live a town life without knowing the reason why;—must live a town life or die a town death. But a woman should not be treated like a dog. (233, vol. 2, chap. 63)

To submit to the man she loves, then, is to give up the autonomy she has enjoyed since she came into her fortune three years before the novel begins. Moreover, the analogy of the dog and its master does not encourage us to view John Grey as sympathetic or Alice as particularly misguided in her rejection of him.

Whereas loving John Grey counts as a negative in Alice's calculations, *not* loving her cousin George allows her to fantasize about participating as a free agent in a purely financial investment. George Vavasor is a stockbroker and would-be radical politician whose financial and political successes are by no means assured. But his appeal is precisely because he offers a risky investment. Alice imagines that investing in George will give her life the excitement that she longs for:

She envied Kate. Kate could, as his sister, attach herself to George's political career, and obtain from it all that excitement of life which Alice desired for herself. Alice could not love her cousin and marry him; but she felt that if she could do so without impropriety she would like to stick close to him like another sister, to spend her money in aiding his career in Parliament as Kate would do. (112, vol. 1, chap. 11)

When Alice agrees to become George's wife, she pictures it as a kind of business relationship. She writes an "acceptance" letter to him in which she claims: "We could not stand up together as man and wife with any hope of a happy marriage, unless we had both agreed that such happiness might be had without passionate love," even as she assures him of her willingness to invest in his political aspirations, avowing that she takes "a livelier interest in [his] career than in any of the other matters around [her]" (338, vol. 1, chap. 32). Dreading the prospect of a marriage to George even as she accepts his proposal, Alice postpones the wedding for one year, but offers a very businesslike arrangement in the interim: "I know ... that your need of assistance from my means is immediate rather than prospective. My money may be absolutely necessary to you within this year, during which, as I tell you most truly, I cannot bring myself to become a married woman" (339, vol. 1, chap. 32). In this way Alice builds a fantasy in which she can negotiate the terms of her relationship with George based on his financial need, her willingness to part with her money, and her unwillingness to invest herself emotionally or physically along with her money.

The horror of Alice's predicament, as it comes to be revealed, is that because she is a woman, there is no investing her capital without investing her person also. Her idea that she could marry George as a business relationship is undone when he demands access to her physical self, which is his right as her future husband:

Was she to give herself bodily,—body and soul, as she said aloud in her solitary agony,—to a man whom she did not love? Must she submit to his caresses,—lie on his bosom,—turn herself warmly to his kisses? "No," she said, "no,"—speaking audibly, as she walked about the room; "no;—it was not in my bargain; I never meant it." But if so what had she meant;—what had been her dream? (382–83, vol. 1, chap. 37)

The world that Alice lives in has no room for a single woman to conduct business that is not the business of falling in love and getting married. It is not that Alice learns that her fantasy of autonomy is unattractive, but rather that, learning it is unfeasible, she is forced to resort to a "lesser of two evils" option. Significantly, this scene of Alice's repentance is one of the most sensational moments in the novel, followed by George's assault on Kate, in which he breaks her arm on the windswept moor and threatens to murder both Alice and her if he doesn't get what he wants, and his assault on John Grey, in which he shoots at him and misses. And the more sensationally villainous George becomes, the more "romantic" John Grey appears.[19]

What allows John Grey to win Alice back is that she gives George access to almost all of her money and, to protect her from being swindled, Grey substitutes his own money for Alice's. By stepping into the financial contract with which Alice has attempted to engage George, Grey rescues her from "poverty, friendlessness, and helplessness" (Cobbe, "What Shall We Do" 87). Alice's position is rendered one of material exigency: Grey offers her, first, financial security, which would have been destroyed when George took the money, and, second, physical safety, when he stands between George and her, preventing, we might infer, an attack similar to the one on Kate. The narrator asks: "Would it not have been well for her to have a master who by his wisdom and strength could have saved her from such wretched doubtings as these?" (358, vol. 1, chap. 34). And the reader is given the opportunity to answer in the affirmative that, yes, it would be better for Alice to be married to a good man who will be "civilly responsible for her acts" and under whose "protection of cover" she can live (Bodichon 6).

Given that some man must be her master, John Grey is clearly a better choice, but *Can Your Forgive Her?* resists making the resolution triumphant:

> Of course she had no choice but to yield. He, possessed of power and force infinitely greater than hers, had left her no alternative but to be happy. But there still clung to her what I fear we must call a perverseness of obstinacy ... And it may be that there was still left within her bosom some remnant of that feeling of rebellion which his masterful spirit had ever produced in her ... She shrank from him, back against the stonework of the embrasure, but she could not shrink away from his grasp. She put her hand up to impede his, but his hand, like his

character and his words, was full of power. It would not be impeded. "Alice," he said, as he pressed her close with his arm, "the battle is over now, and I have won it."

"You win everything,—always," she said, whispering to him, as she still shrank from his embrace. (355, vol. 2, chap. 74)

This happy resolution, such as it is, clearly shows that Alice's near-hysterical aversion to giving herself emotionally and physically to her fiancé has not abated and that she has been conquered rather than persuaded. The question of the novel's title, therefore, seems to operate on a couple of different registers, asking not only whether the reader can forgive Alice for doing rash, perverse things that jeopardize herself and her fortune, but also whether the reader can forgive the novel itself for making it hard to buy into Alice's happy ending. The forgiveness that the novel asks of its readers for Alice herself may be for the domestic tragedy that she threatens to bring to her family and friends by throwing herself and her money away on George's political "cause."[20] But if Alice's potential tragedy seems precipitated by fiction that Trollope is at great pains to designate "safe," then it is unclear if his own novel has furthered the cause of "love-making" or if, instead, it has left in its readers, as in Alice, "some remnant of that feeling of rebellion" which impelled her to resist the marriage plot.

MISS MACKENZIE: "THE BEAUTY OF A HIGH RATE OF INTEREST"

Mr. Trollope has taken the trouble to execute a very skilful photograph of a number of exceedingly tedious and unpleasant people, in order to show that vulgarity, and middle-age, and dulness are none of them incompatible with a good deal of sound sentiment. The indisputable truth of the implied conclusions scarcely compensates for the stupidity and downright unpleasantness of the people who have been introduced to us in order to illustrate the truth.

—Review of *Miss Mackenzie*, *Saturday Review* (1865)

Published in two volumes the same year that *Can You Forgive Her?* was appearing in serial form, *Miss Mackenzie* describes the problem of an independent woman with capital. The novel is about an aging spinster who inherits the fortune of her invalid brother (whom she has nursed for fifteen years) once he dies. When the novel opens, the prosaic heroine, Miss Margaret Mackenzie, is thirty-four years old and "neither beautiful nor clever" (4), but with a clandestine attachment to poetry and romance and a fortune large enough to give her "eight hundred a year" (13), she sets out to get the best happiness that her money can buy. She is approached by four suitors who find her eight hundred attractive: Harry Handcock, who exits the plot early on; Samuel Rubb, junior, the son of her brother's business partner, a dealer in oilcloths who is good-looking and young but vulgar (with a predilection for bright-yellow gloves and oiled hair); Jeremiah Maguire, a clergyman who is a gentleman but who also has a disfiguring squint; and her cousin Sir John Ball, who is an old, bald, and penny-pinching widower with nine children. Margaret seems first to incline to Samuel Rubb, who, though he is vulgar, might offer her romance, but eventually she learns to love Sir John Ball. When the fortune is discovered to belong not to Margaret, but to Sir John, he romantically asks her to marry him for love and not for money. Mr. Maguire becomes the villain of the piece when he hounds Margaret and Sir John, pretending that he is engaged to her already and publishing libelous letters about Sir John's predations on the innocent heiress, until he is finally discredited. Ultimately, Margaret is relieved to give up her fortune, which has caused her so much trouble, and to become Lady Ball "thankfully, quietly, and with an enduring satisfaction as became such a woman to do" (401).

On the surface, Margaret and Alice seem to have opposite problems: Margaret calculates her chances at the kind of romance and love she has read about in novels, whereas Alice flees from precisely that romance and love for "some vague idea that there was something to be done; a something above and beyond, or perhaps altogether beside that marrying and having two children" (*Can You Forgive Her?* 110, vol. 1, chap. 11). Yet in their nascent desires to exercise agency, they pursue similarly speculative investments. Margaret speculates on her chances for romance, eschewing the safe investments that will offer security but little "interest."

In the first chapter of *Miss Mackenzie*, Margaret rejects Harry Handcock, the friend of her late brother, who proposes to her in a "short and sensible" letter, of which the narrator says: "As to her money he told her that no doubt he regarded it now as a great addition to their chance of happiness, should they put their lots together" (12). Margaret, however, has "strong aspirations": "She thought, or rather hoped, that society might still open to her its portals—not simply the society of the Handcocks from Somerset House, but that society of which she had read in novels during the day, and of which she had dreamed at night"(13). She likewise rejects her cousin's first offer because "he was very careworn, soiled as it were with the world," because "of romance in him there was nothing left," and because "it would be very sad to be the wife of such a man" (111). Margaret's desire for something better is, not surprisingly, couched in terms of novel-reading—novels that she consumes in daily doses and that shape her dreams and desires for more and similar romance.

Moreover, she is not just a consumer but also a producer of romance. The narrator tells us of the existence of

> quires of manuscript in which Margaret had written her thoughts and feelings—hundreds of rhymes which had never met any eye but her own; and outspoken words of love contained in letters which had never been sent, or been intended to be sent, to any destination. Indeed these letters had been commenced with no name, and finished with no signature … No one had ever guessed all this, or had dreamed of accusing Margaret of romance. (9)

In these love letters with no sender and no recipient, Margaret has created a romantic narrative into which the inheritance finally allows her to insert herself. She then auditions, often humorously, the men in her life for the role of "leading man." When, for example, she imagines the Reverend Maguire as her lover, she is troubled by his divergence from her literary ideal:

> As soon as he was gone she remembered that his name was Jeremiah … If [the marriage] did come to pass how was she to call him? She tried the entire word Jeremiah, but it did not seem to answer. She tried Jerry also, but that was worse. Jerry might have been very well had they come together fifteen years earlier in life, but she did not think that she could call him Jerry now. She supposed it must be Mr. Maguire; but if so, half the romance of the thing would be gone at once! (172)

Margaret's musings on the fitness of Mr. Maguire for the role of romantic hero signal the novel's own play with the genre of the romance. How unromantic a romance can Margaret stand? Can she accept Mr. Maguire's squint or his inelegant name? How unromantic a romance can the reader stand?

But Margaret's desire for romance first leads her to an investment both financial and romantic. Within her first weeks at Littlebath, she receives a business letter from her brother asking for the loan of £2,400 and promising her the mortgage to the business as security. The letter announces that Mr. Samuel Rubb, junior, will come visit her to explain the affair. The narrator's description of Margaret's reaction to her brother's proposal looks very similar to the description of Alexander Shand's widow with her small inheritance to invest:

> Like all other single ladies, she was very nervous about her money. She was quite alive to the beauty of a high rate of interest, but did not quite understand that high interest and impaired security should go hand in hand together ... She knew that lone women were terribly robbed sometimes, and had almost resolved upon insisting [to her lawyers] that the money should be put into the Three per Cents. But she had gone to work with figures, and having ascertained that by doing so twenty-five pounds a year would be docked off her computed income, she had given no such order. She now again went to work with her figures, and found that if the loan were accomplished it would add twenty-five pounds a year to her computed income. (36–37)

If Margaret, preinheritance, has spent her energies producing and consuming romantic poetry and novels, postinheritance she expands her oeuvre to include financial computations. It is not that she has become less romantic, but that the possibilities of a lucrative investment exercise the same sensational appeal for her as her novels and poetry once did.

Likewise, when Samuel Rubb arrives, his attractions for Margaret are clearly a combination of the sexual and the economic. Although she is initially inclined to be snobbish, because he is not a gentleman, she finds that he is dignified after all, authoritative and good-looking, and that "there was certainly no knowing that he belonged to the oilcloth business from the cut of his coat or the set of his trousers" (37–38). And his "pitch" is equally persuasive:

> By the time that Mr. Samuel Rubb had done, Miss Mackenzie found herself to have dismounted altogether from her [high] horse, and to be pervaded by some slight fear that her lawyers might allow so favorable an opportunity for investing her money to slip through their hands.

Then, on a sudden, Mr. Rubb dropped the subject of the loan, and Miss Mackenzie, as he did so, felt herself to be almost disappointed. And when she found him talking easily to her about matters of external life, although she answered him readily, and talked to him also easily, she entertained some feeling that she ought to be offended … Nevertheless, Miss Mackenzie answered him when he asked questions, and allowed herself to be seduced into a conversation. (38)

Even more than his prepossessing appearance, Mr. Rubb's business talk woos Margaret. Or it might be more accurate to say that the sexual and the financial attractions of Mr. Samuel Rubb, junior, are indistinguishable to her. Mr. Rubb represents just what one wants from a speculative investment: the potential of a big future payoff. Compared to the failed Sir John, "[Rubb] was not worn out with life; he was not broken with care; he would look forward into the world, and hope for things to come" (112).

Mr. Rubb's appeal, strangely, is not mitigated when Margaret learns from her lawyer that she doesn't have the security on the mortgage and that Rubb has swindled her out of her £2,400. When Mr. Rubb himself follows the lawyer's letter to do damage control, Trollope highlights the combination of confessed swindle and seduction:

He came close to her, hesitated for a moment, and then, putting one hand behind her waist, though barely touching her, he took her hand with his other hand. She thought that he was going to kiss her lips, and for a moment or two he thought so too … As it was, he merely raised her hand and kissed that. When she could look into his face his eyes were full of tears …

"[T]he fact is you could sell us up if you pleased. I didn't mean it when I first got your brother to agree as to asking you for the loan; I didn't indeed; but things were going wrong with us, and just at that moment they went more wrong than ever; and then came the temptation … ."

This was all true, but how far the truth should be taken towards palliating the deed done, I must leave the reader to decide; and the reader will doubtless perceive that the truth did not appear until Mr. Rubb had ascertained that its appearance would not injure him … The tear which he rubbed from his eye with his hand counted very much in his favor with Miss Mackenzie; she had not only forgiven him now, but she almost loved him for having given her something to forgive. (130–31)

The scene is a complex one, in which the reader (despite Trollope's claim that he will "leave us to decide") is clearly prompted to see Mr. Rubb as a scoundrel, but is also given to understand that Mr. Rubb, "having something real in his heart, having some remnant of generous feeling left about him" (131), is prevented from pushing his advantage with Margaret. She forgives him, I think, because even (or especially) if he is a dangerous investment, he offers her a sensational and dramatic interest. Trollope's cynical observation that "with many women I doubt whether there be any more effectual way of touching their hearts than ill-using them and then confessing it" (131) might be read less as describing Margaret's self-abnegation than as describing her desire for drama and excitement; betrayal and reconciliation are more exciting than reliability and comfort.

But even if Mr. Rubb is clearly a bad investment for Margaret, he is not entirely unsympathetic to the reader. And, equally, the "worthy man" of the novel, Sir John, does not present a particularly sound investment for the heroine. In addition to being bald and careworn, he is described in the novel as having ludicrous and sinister financial preoccupations:

> He had some small capital—some remnant of his father's trade wealth, which he nursed with extreme care, buying shares here and there as his keen outlook into City affairs directed him. I do not suppose that he had much talent for the business, or he would have grown rich ... He was always thinking of his money; excusing himself to himself and to others by the fact of his nine children. For myself I think that his children were no justification to him; as they would have been held to be none, had he murdered and robbed his neighbors for their sake. (75)

Far from representing the fitness of men to rule the financial realm (as opposed to Margaret's imprudent assay at investing), Sir John, who "nurses" his capital along with his nine children, appears emasculated by his financial dealings. Nevertheless, the narrator's reference to murdering and robbing also imbues Sir John with a kind of sensational negative appeal; he is, we gather, both ruthless and ineffectual.

The shift in the novel by which Sir John becomes the romantic hero amounts to a sleight of hand on Trollope's part. By flashing the increasingly unsympathetic Mr. Maguire (with his terrible squint) and Mr. Rubb with his vulgar yellow gloves and perfumed and oiled hair in front of the reader, the novel gradually becomes kinder to Sir John. We are privy, for instance, to this reckoning by Margaret: "For, after all, she thought she liked him best of all the men and women that she knew. He was always in trouble, but then she fancied that with him she at any rate knew the worst. There was nothing concealed with him—nothing to be afraid of" (187). The humorously sensational horror of Mr. Rubb's social faux pas and Mr. Maguire's more genuinely dangerous debts and dishonesty make the "known evil" of Sir John—his ruthlessness and his ineptitude—seem less unpleasant.

But the main shift in the novel from Margaret feeling "it would be very sad to be the wife of such a man" (111) to the end, when she tells him, "I love you better than all the world besides" (393) is the difference between eight hundred a year and nothing a year. When the money is her own, Margaret considers a marriage to Sir John a sacrifice of herself and "what she ha[s] left of her youth" (110), but when he proposes to her after she has lost her fortune, and she accepts, the narrator tells us:

> It was not only, nor even chiefly, that she who, on the preceding morning, had awakened to the remembrance of her utter destitution, now felt that all those terrible troubles were over. It was not simply that her great care had been vanquished for her. It was this, that the man who had a second time come to her asking for her love, had now given her all-sufficient evidence that he did so for the sake of her love. (276)

By repeating twice Margaret's rescue from destitution, the passage highlights what it purports to discount—her pecuniary interests in Sir John—but it is also precisely the moment in the novel when we are allowed to reinvest in the romance plot.

If we, like Margaret, can buy the "all-sufficient" evidence that love conquers all, then we will have invested in Trollope's love story, and we will have learned the lesson that it strives to teach us: it is better to be rescued as a damsel in distress than to be an independent heiress attempting to make correct assessments of her opportunities. In fact, shortly before Margaret loses her fortune, she begins to wish it away:

> Since her brother's death, three men had offered to marry her, and there was a fourth from whom she had expected such an offer. She

looked upon all this with dismay, and told herself that she was not fit to sail, under her own guidance, out in the broad sea, amidst such rocks as those ... Had she not always been ill at ease, and out of her element, while striving at Littlebath to live the life of a lady of fortune? (191)

Miss Mackenzie echoes the narrator's question in *Can You Forgive Her?*: "Would it not have been well for her to have a master who by his wisdom and strength could have saved her from such wretched doubtings as these?" (358, vol. 1, chap. 34).

Margaret's anxiety about choosing which of her four suitors is the best investment of her money and her self is alleviated when her investment shrinks to only herself. As a penniless spinster, in other words, she has less to lose and more to gain by a marriage to Sir John. Like the conclusion of *Can You Forgive Her?*, *Miss Mackenzie* allows the reader to buy into the romance plot by presenting financial perils from which the heroine must be rescued. Thus the very venal concerns that we understand as antithetical to "true love" become the vehicle for the reader to reinvest in the love story. The promises held out to the reader may, on even cursory inspection, look shady, unreliable, even dangerous, but as Alexander Shand remarks, "People must invest."

THE STRUGGLES OF BROWN, JONES, AND ROBINSON: "CREDIT AND CREDIT ONLY WAS REQUIRED"

We deeply regret, for Mr. Trollope's own reputation, that 'The Struggles of Brown, Jones, and Robinson' should have been published. It was universally felt, when the story first appeared in the 'Cornhill Magazine,' that the whole affair was a blunder.

—Review of *The Struggles of Brown, Jones, and Robinson*,
Westminster Review (1871)

If Trollope treated his novels as investment opportunities for his readers, then his "deformed child," *The Struggles of Brown, Jones, and Robinson*, seemingly never offered a convincing prospectus to its investors. This, I argue, is not because it offers his most unadorned version of realism, but because it presents his most complexly theoretical and self-reflexive account of the role of fiction. The sales pitch of the fictional memoir's author, George Robinson, in presenting the novel itself as "a new article" with "nothing equal to it at the price at present on the market" (10) seems to exemplify the commodification of Trollope's fiction. Yet the novel offers a sophisticated account and critique of the production of belief that is mandated by the logic of both the Victorian economic exchange system and the sexual exchange system of the novel. The novel makes humorously explicit what is, I contend, implicit in Victorian realism in general: the realist novel's project is the production of belief in a "real" that has no referent but that is itself crucial to the operation of the systems of exchange in which it participates and which it describes. Robinson is the ad man for his firm, and as such he understands himself as a producer of narrative, but not narrative-as-commodity. Robinson understands his work, rather, as participating in a credit economy, wherein the actual commodities and the capital associated with them are less important than the *belief* in them. As he explains in the preface:

> That bugbear Capital is a crumbling old tower, and is pretty nigh brought to its last ruin. Credit is the polished shaft of the temple on which the new world of trade will be content to lean. That I take is the one great doctrine of modern commerce. Credit,—credit,—credit. Get credit, and capital will follow. Doesn't the word speak for itself? Must not credit be respectable? (4)

Ironically, too, Robinson links this symbolic credit directly to domestic romance when he plays with the multiple meanings of the word *credit:*

> Capital, though it's a bugbear, nevertheless it's a virtue. Therefore, as you haven't got it, you must assume it. That's credit. Credit I take to be the belief of other people in a thing that doesn't really exist. When you go into your friend Smith's house and find Mrs. S. all smiles, you give her credit for the sweetest of tempers. Your friend S. knows better; but then you see she's had wit enough to obtain credit. When I draw a bill at three months and get it done, I do the same thing. That's credit. (7)

Just as Mrs. Smith's assumption of good temper generates a belief in her as an Angel in the House, so Robinson's assumption of the appearance of capital instills a belief in him as a paragon of economic virtue.

Robinson earns credit in this "new world of trade" by writing sensational advertising copy that has virtually no reference to either real capital or real commodities, which he himself admits: "To obtain credit the only certain method is to advertise. Advertise, advertise, advertise. That is, assume, assume, assume. Go on assuming your virtue. The more you haven't got it, the more you must assume it" (7). The advertising flyers that Robinson produces in the service of the partners' fledgling haberdashery business—gorgeous descriptions of fantastic merchandise at cut-rate prices, sensational bulletins about the status of villainous wholesale dealers, lurid reports of "three suckling infants ... pressed to death in their mothers' arms" by a crowd of overeager shoppers (200)—bear little or no resemblance to actual commodities or events. But they tell stories that establish the firm's credit and credibility with the public.

Robinson advertises, in other words, not the commodities available to the public, but the image of a firm that provides luxury commodities to the public. For example, he "invents" a Katakairion shirt as a marketing ploy that he must then explain to his partners:

"If that isn't swindling, I don't know what is," said Jones.

"Do you know what Katakairion means?" said Robinson.

"No; I don't," said Jones. "And I don't want to know."

"Katakairion means 'fitting,'" said Robinson; "and the purchaser has only to take care that the shirt he buys does fit, and then it is a Katakairion."

"But we didn't invent them."

"We invented the price and the name, and that's as much as anybody does. But that is not all. It's a well-understood maxim in trade, that a man may advertise what he chooses. We advertise to attract notice, not to state facts." (139)

The downfall of the firm, which the memoir chronicles, stems in large part from Brown's and Jones's inability to grasp that there need not be, indeed can't be, any actual reference to "real" items in their business. As we learn, Mr. Brown's insistence on spending "ready money" on some small amount of stock for the store's opening is "a suicidal act on his part":

Credit and credit only was required. But of all modes of extinguishing credit, of crushing, as it were, the young baby in its cradle, there is none equal to that of spending a little ready money, and then halting. In trade as in love, to doubt,—or rather, to seem to doubt,—is to be lost. When you order goods, do so as though the bank were at your back. Look your victim full in the face, and write down your long numbers without a falter in your pen. And should there seem a hesitation on his part, do not affect to understand it. (44–45)

In other words, there may be no "5,000 Kolinski and Minx Boas" in stock (42), but everyone must appear to believe that there are for the system of trade to function. Likewise, true love may not conquer all, but "to appear to doubt" is fatal to the system of sexual exchange.

One could argue, indeed, that the revulsion Trollope's reviewers expressed at *The Struggles of Brown, Jones, and Robinson* is precisely because the novel, like a magician revealing trade secrets, "appears to doubt" its own narrative function. It does not, finally, show love's triumph. Robinson's "true love," Maryanne Brown, is mercenary and hard from beginning to end. Moreover, the one marriage that does occur at the end of the novel, between Robinson's ex-rival for Maryanne, the butcher William Brisket, and a drover's daughter, is a happy ending of the most prosaic nature. As Brisket tells George: "She had three hundred, down, you know;—really down. So I said done and done, when I found the money wasn't there with Maryanne. And I think that I've seen my way" (247).

The "happy" ending of *The Struggles,* inasmuch as it can be said to have one, refers self-reflexively to Robinson's successes as a producer of narrative, when, on the strength of his advertising skill, he is commissioned by the editor of the *Cornhill Magazine*—the magazine in which *The Struggles* actually first appeared serially—to write an "account of the doings of the firm" because "it may be of advantage to commerce in general" (239). Thus, Trollope self-referentially asks his readers to invest in a narrative that tells the story of its own inception—a narrative about the production of narrative.

Although the novel ends with its own beginning, with Robinson at last producing a "real" commodity for public consumption, it is clear that this is not the end point of his endeavors: "George Robinson, though his present wants were provided for by his pen, was by no means disposed to sink into a literary hack. It was by commerce that he desired to shine. It was to trade,—trade, in the highest sense of the word,—that his ambition led him" (250). Robinson, suffering an existential crisis at the end of the novel, ponders failure in trade:

> First he took from his pocket a short list which he always carried, and once more read over the names and figures which it bore.
>
> Barlywig, £40,000 per annum.
>
> How did Barlywig begin such an outlay as that? He knew that Barlywig had, as a boy, walked up to town with twopence in his pocket, and in his early days, had swept out the shop of a shoemaker. The giants of trade all have done that. Then he went on with the list:—

Holloway .	.	.	.	£30,000 per annum.
Moses	.	.	.	10,000 "
Macassar Oil	.	.	.	10,000 "
Dr. De Jongh	.	.	.	10,000 "

> What a glorious fraternity! There were many others that followed with figures almost equally stupendous. Revalenta Arabica! Bedsteads! Paletots! Food for Cattle! But then how did these great men begin? He himself had begun with some money in hand, and he had failed. As to them, he believed that they had all begun with twopence. (249–50)

Robinson's list, which tracks not yearly income but yearly advertising expenses, does several things: Certainly the list looks a little like Trollope's own *An Autobiography*, which famously ends with the list of his novels and the money he received for each—a life's successes recorded in creative outlay and compensation. But, more than that, it evokes a stock portfolio with companies, variously exotic and prosaic, that may or may not be "real" companies dealing in "real" commodities—like Ferdinand Lopez's speculations in the guano trade or Augustus Melmotte's Mexican Railroad—but that are so great as to spend fortunes in advertising alone. Finally, it presents highly sensationalized accounts of the "glorious fraternity"; like Horatio Alger, they have all "begun with twopence" and risen to greatness. The "rags to riches" stories are ones that Robinson himself is heavily invested in.

In *An Autobiography*, a chronicle very much about the novels he wrote, Trollope describes the book he never wrote:

88 / CHAPTER TWO

I intended to write that book to vindicate my own profession as a novelist, and also to vindicate that public taste in literature which has created and nourished the profession which I follow. And I was stirred up to make such an attempt by a conviction that there still exists among us Englishmen a prejudice in respect to novels which might, perhaps, be lessened by such a work. This prejudice is not against the reading of novels, as is proved by their general acceptance among us. But it exists strongly in reference to the appreciation in which they are professed to be held; and it robs them of much of that high character which they may claim to have earned by their grace, their honesty, and good teaching. (196–97)

It may be fanciful to say that *The Struggles of Brown, Jones, and Robinson* is that book; nonetheless, I believe that the desire to vindicate fiction writing that Trollope articulates here and elsewhere is expressed as an ambivalence in *The Struggles* that is not, as critics have remarked, about "the equation between money and fiction" (Brantlinger, *Reading Lesson* 121) but about Trollope's own participation, like George Robinson, in an economy of credit, in the production of belief: advertising "to attract notice, not to state facts."

Trollope understands his fiction as doing real things in the real world—as exercising a kind of discursive power over readers, for good or ill. In "On English Prose Fiction as a Rational Amusement," Trollope questions the writer's ethical responsibility:

Simple success in a profession,—by which I mean the making of money or the gaining of a reputation,—cannot be sufficient for any man or woman with a conscience. Labour that is useless,—unproductive,—will break the heart of a convict. Do you believe it possible then that an enlightened man,—one, at least, so far enlightened as to be able to produce for you pictures of life that shall delight you,—can do so from year to year, contentedly, without a self-inquiry whether he be producing any good by his work,—without at least satisfying himself that he does not produce evil? (96)

Likewise, as Robinson ponders his ethical responsibility, he too questions the productivity of his own work:

"Why don't you produce something, so as to make the world richer?" Poppins had said. He knew well what Poppins had meant by making the world richer. If a man invent a Katakairion shirt, he does make the world richer; if it be a good one, he makes it much richer. But the man who simply says that he has done so adds nothing to the world's wealth ... Was a man bound to produce true shirts for the world's benefit even though he should make no money by so doing;—either true shirts or none at all? (252–53)

In Trollope's case, the anxiety is not that his novels are commodities, but that they are *not*. And if his labor does not produce "true" Katakairion shirts, but only the belief in them, should he then produce "none at all"?

Robinson ends up in a position similar to Trollope's own, for as Robinson worries that his work may not be productive, he hears a message in the chiming of church bells, as if from heaven: "Turn again, Robinson, Member of Parliament" (254). His faith in the power of his work to produce a "real" product is renewed—that product: himself as a man of consequence in the political world. It is well-known that Trollope himself stood, unsuccessfully, for a seat in Parliament, but I don't wish to stress the connections between Robinson's and his personal aspirations. Rather, I want to return to Trollope's claim that Dickens's novels will "help to make many women." This is the "real" product of Trollope's writing, not the "dainty dishes" of novels for consumption but actual social and political effects in the world—in fact, real men and women.

Trollope's critics have often imagined his work as inviting a turn from sensational romance to the "faithful portraiture" of real life; that is, the reader's investments are transferred from romantic unrealities to the scientific satisfactions of seeing "life as it really is." But this experiment overstepped its bounds, which is clear in a reviewer's comment about *The Struggles of Brown, Jones, and Robinson*:

The chief characters, motives, and incidents were so odiously vulgar and stupid that the staunchest champions of realism were forced to give it up in disgust. It may be questioned whether any living being ever got to the end of *Brown, Jones, and Robinson*, or had any other sentiment than mingled loathing or despair towards that weary tribe of butchers and drapers, and their still more wearisome wives. (Review of *Miss Mackenzie, Saturday Review* 216)

In other words, realism is good insofar as it eschews "sensation poison" in favor of "homogeneous and consistent pictures" (Hoey 400), but it is bad insofar as its detailed pictures of ugly reality make affective attachments impossible.

Yet, as I have argued in this chapter, Trollope offers his readers a very different dynamic, whereby investments in "vulgar" empirical observations (or perhaps one might say empirical observations of vulgar "characters, motives and incidents") initiate and sustain the reader's sensational attachments. Venal quotidian concerns are rendered suspenseful and romantic. In *Can You Forgive Her?* and *Miss Mackenzie,* the reader's knowledge of the world "as it really is"—an aging spinster with a very small fortune may have some latitude in choosing what to do with herself and her money, but none of her choices are likely to be very good ones—is ultimately superceded by the reader's belief in the world "as it is not": true love chooses you if you can suffer patiently long enough. Thus, ironically, Trollope's unveiling of the "man behind the curtain," which Henry James found so appalling, serves to earn credit *for the romances* that he tells. Moreover, by inviting readers to buy into romances that look like bad investments, these novels highlight the process through which the objects of our empirical knowledge can become imbued with sentimental belief.

And, as I will show in the next chapter, it is this investment in the promises of sentiment and romance that George Meredith invites his readers to question in *The Egoist* and *Diana of the Crossways.* If Trollope's novels demonstrate that critical distance must, in the final analysis, be suspended for the social myths to do their work, then Meredith, in asking his readers to consider exactly what payoff they get from attachment to those myths, offers a much more complicated position that not only claims critical acumen but also owns its sensational susceptibility. In this way, Meredith asks his reader to turn a critical eye on his or her own most cherished attachments—attachments not just to romance, but to one's own sophisticated immunity to romance.

CHAPTER THREE

The "New Fiction" Theorizes Cultural Consumption

And yet there can be no doubt that, even judged by his novels alone, Meredith re-mains a great writer. The doubt is rather whether he can be called a great novelist; whether, indeed, anyone to whom the technique of novel writing had so much that was repulsive in it can excel compared with those who are writing, not against the grain, but with it. He struggles to escape, and the chapters of amazing but fruitless energy which he produces in his struggle to escape are the true obstacles to the enjoy-ment of Meredith. What, we ask is he struggling against? What is he striving for?

　—Virginia Woolf, "On Re-Reading Meredith" (1928)

The time may hereafter arrive, in far distant years, when the population of the earth shall be kept as strictly within the bounds of number and suitability of race, as sheep on a well-ordered moor or the plants in an orchard house; in the meantime, let us do what we can to encourage the multiplication of the races best fitted to invent and conform to a high and generous civilization.

　—Francis Galton, *Hereditary Genius* (1869)

If there is one thing that George Meredith's critics agree on, it is that reading him is hard work. Not only do his novels defy generic cate-gorization, but they are also "difficult"; they thwart identification, in some cases pleasure, in many cases interpretation. As one reviewer writes of *Diana of the Crossways* in the *Pall Mall Gazette* in 1885:

In reading Mr George Meredith one is perpetually divided between admiration for his genius and irritation at his perversity. The genius was always there, but the perversity increases. Mr Meredith has a theory of his own about style, and the more evident it becomes that

91

consistent adherence to that theory makes him unreadable to ordinary mortals, the more pertinaciously, defiantly he develops it. (265)

In particular, Meredith strains his reader's patience and attention in the prefatory chapters of his novels, as if one were required to pass a test to enter into the rest of the novel. Gayla McGlamery describes such chapters this way: "Several of these ... are so turgid as to appear almost confrontational. Instead of proffering the customary lures to further reading, they tempt readers to ignore, or skim over them" ("Malady" 331).[1]

However, this "confrontational" writing style that dares its readers *not* to read lies at the heart of Meredith's literary innovation and cultural critique. By insisting on the *work* of reading, Meredith inaugurates a new kind reader, and a new relationship to the novel, in which the pleasures of reading are explicitly the pleasures of critical acumen and resistance to the emotional pull of sensational or sentimental tropes. In challenging the generic boundaries of the novel, Meredith unmasks the iniquities masquerading as romance in the relationship between the sexes. Using Meredith's *The Egoist* as an exemplar, Henry Holbeach (W. B. Rands) writes in his 1880 essay "The New Fiction":

> Within the last twenty years the novel proper has undergone a development which may still be pronounced astonishing even by those who have been accustomed to consider it, and has taken rank side by side ... with poetry and philosophy, formally so entitled ... It may almost be said that there is now a branch of criticism specially, if not exclusively, applying to novels; and, perhaps, it may be added that the critics who cultivate this branch of work do not yet feel themselves quite up to their work. In fact, the New Fiction is a product for which the canons were not ready. (150)

Holbeach imagines fiction like Meredith's as having evolved (although, given his amazement at the rapidity of the change, it might be more accurate to say "mutated") into a "serious" genre, but he also imagines the New Fiction demanding an evolution in critical thought about what the novel does. Meredith's fiction is therefore viewed (and views itself) at the vanguard of culture, participating in the evolution of "art" and, through "art," society.

Critics have tended to stress Meredith's "scientific" qualities—to consider him a post-Darwinian novelist, whose use of Darwin's theories of natural and sexual selection challenges the social violence of gender inequality and undermines the novel's traditional faith in romance.[2] Yet I argue that Meredith's social critique is more complicated than that. Not only does he highlight the dangers of subjugating women for the future evolution of the "race," but he also links that subjugation directly to what women (and men) read and how they read it. In this chapter I consider two of Meredith's novels, *The Egoist* (1879) and *Diana of the Crossways* (1885), both of which offer feminist critiques of Woman's plight in a society that simultaneously sentimentalizes and denigrates the feminine. I maintain, however, that both novels, in addition to calling for "evolutionary" advance in the relationship between the sexes, imagine that the woman reader herself is crucially linked to that evolution. Meredith reminds his readers that the critical detachment on which they congratulate themselves is painfully elusive. Sensational investments are inescapable, and the seeming objectivity that science proffers must, therefore, be suspect.

In *The Egoist*'s turgid prelude, for example, Meredith's narrator sets up the novel's combined critique of the objective science of evolution and the objective art of literary realism. He says of realism: "The realistic method of a conscientious transcription of all the visible, and a repetition of all the audible, is mainly accountable for our present branfulness, and that prolongation of the vasty and the noisy, out of which, as from an undrained fen, steams the malady of sameness, our modern malady" (34). The belief that this moral and aesthetic malaise can be remedied by new scientific knowledge is, the narrator informs us, a gross mistake:

> We drove in a body to Science the other day for an antidote; which was as if tired pedestrians should mount the engine-box of headlong trains; and Science introduced us to our o'er-hoary ancestry—them in Oriental posture; whereupon we set up a primeval chattering to rival the Amazon forest nigh nightfall, cured, we fancied. And before daybreak our disease was hanging on to us again, with the extension of a tail … We were the same, and animals into the bargain. That is all we got from Science. (34)

In other words, the novel warns its readers to be suspicious of the very answers that the novel itself seems to provide in its adoption of evolutionary rhetoric as unifying thread and narrative device. Indeed, as the quote suggests, literary realism and scientific positivism are both driven by a similarly misplaced faith in progressive action, "headlong trains." Instead, Meredith offers a blended critique of scientific and narrative progress that is infused in the novel's "flaws," in its interruptions of narrative action, its refusals of generic expectations.

Similarly, the preface of *Diana of the Crossways* presents the novel itself as an interpretive dilemma. The novel, which is the fictionalized account of real-life "witty Beauty" Caroline Norton, begins with the chapter "Of Diaries and Diarists Touching the Heroine," in which the narrator offers an introduction to Diana and her high-profile scandal through the accounts of various fictional diarists. The Diarists' accounts, we learn, are incomplete, biased, and in most cases representative of a savage, gossip-mongering world, which the narrator describes thus:

> It does not pretend to know the whole, or naked body of the facts; it knows enough for its fumy dubiousness; and excepting the sentimental of men, a rocket-headed horde, ever at the heels of fair faces for ignition, and up starring away at a hint of tearfulness;—excepting further by chance a solid champion man, or some generous woman capable of faith in the pelted solitary of her sex, our temporary world blows direct East on her shivering person. (3)

The novel asks its readers to be better readers than those who condemn a woman unfairly, or who speculate on her guilt or innocence with incomplete information. As the narrator says, "It is a test of the civilized to see and hear, and add no yapping to the spectacle" (7). *Diana* offers, then, the illusion of "history," of filling in the gaps that the Diarists leave, revealing the "naked body" of the famous scandal and its main actors. But it also provides a comfortable sense that, having sympathized with its heroine, one is free of the prejudices of the "yapping" hounds.[3] However, as the quote above suggests, sympathizing for the wrong reasons—simply because the woman *is* sympathetic—is little better than condemning her out of hand. The sentimental men are still part of the pack at Diana's heels, after all.

Yet the novel encourages the very sensational and sentimental reading that it criticizes. For instance, one reviewer notes that the novel's appeal lies in its exciting "real-life" subject matter:

> Such a career as that of his Diana might well bring down upon his head the charge of extravagance if he could not point to well-known

facts in support of its most startling incidents. Diana's beauty and wit; her social, literary, and political power; her unfortunate early marriage; her dangerous intimacy with a distinguished statesman, and the consequent scandal; her betrayal of an important Cabinet secret; the failure of her husband's attempt to obtain a divorce—all these are facts, and quite sufficient to form the basis of a very "sensational" novel. (Monkhouse 262)

Moreover, the novel takes liberties with its subject that increase rather than palliate the very sentimentalizing that it criticizes; it offers a version of Caroline Norton rendered more "comic" than the original by the subtraction of Norton's children and the tragic custody battles that she fought for them and by the addition of a suitable marriage to a passionate, wealthy, and ultramanly lover while Diana is still young and beautiful.[4] Even as the novel advocates clear-sighted Philosophy—a term that Meredith uses very much like Comedy in *The Egoist* to signify moral and aesthetic advance in culture—it suggests that it is impossible for readers not to read sensationally.

The Egoist and *Diana* are "comedies" with the requisite romance plots and marriage resolutions, yet the romances and marriages that they offer are problematic at best. The tension between social critique and narrative satisfaction, however, is precisely where both offer their most trenchant appraisals of cultural (re)production and consumption. This critique might be described, at its most basic, as a deep anxiety about the conjunction of sex and culture or, to put it another way, about the conjunction of breeding and breeding.[5]

Critics have typically reckoned the concerns of the Victorian social scientists and reformers as antithetical to those of the cultural, aesthetic elite. As the century drew to a close, so the argument goes, the division of intellectual labor pushed literature and art farther from the public sphere, forcing a retreat of "serious" art from the vulgar demands of consumer culture and "the masses." For example, T. W. Heyck writes:

As the size of the literate public grew, especially from the 1860s on, and as cheap literature for the masses poured from the presses, serious writers such as Meredith, Hardy, and Gissing sensed that there had come into existence an audience about which they knew little and with which they had no sympathy. Thus the doctrine of "art-for-art's-sake," clearly established as the ideology of the most advanced artists in England by the 1870s, was both a reaction against the values of the middle-class reader and a revulsion from a new audience with which they had little contact or sympathy. It was an attempt to restore order to the world of serious literature by compressing the responsibilities and audience of art to a manageable perimeter. (176–77)[6]

Yet Meredith, far from "compressing" art's responsibilities or audience, conceives of aesthetic production and consumption as crucial to the progress of "the race," an *expansion* of responsibility made possible in the latter decades of the nineteenth century by the rise of social Darwinist thought. For Meredith, the seriousness of being a "serious writer" lies not in alienating the philistine reading public with inaccessible, "highbrow" literature, but in *cultivating* an improved reading public.

Meredith suggests a couple of things for literary scholarship considered in this way: First, the familiar vision of an elevated, isolated modernist aesthetic may not necessarily repudiate the socially engaged didacticism of the Victorian literary market; rather, the "literati at the margins" stance of the modernists (by way of the aesthetes and decadents) may define an ethically responsible relationship of the artist—as cultural critic and prophet—to the *educable* masses. As Virginia Woolf writes of the reader's responsibilities to know bad books from good: "Are they not the most insidious enemies of society, corrupters, defilers, the writers of false books, faked books, books that fill the air with decay and disease? Let us then be severe in our judgments; let us compare each book with the greatest of its kind" ("How Should One Read a Book?" 8–9). Woolf argues that the readers, with tastes shaped by their understanding of "the greatest" books, are in duty bound to judge what they read with "the rarest qualities of imagination, insight and judgment" and that "we have our responsibilities as readers and even our importance" (11). In other words, the modernist aesthetic ideal may be the personal, psychological, and individual (as opposed to the social, didactic, and moral), but this ideal is urged on readers who must learn to appreciate and emulate it, so that they may resist "the enemies of society."[7]

Second, in stressing the necessity of cultivated critical reading and of examining the cultural embedment of literary production and consumption, Meredith's social-aesthetic imperative suggests itself as a precursor to current critical practice in a way that both acknowledges and critiques the seductive appeal of imagining the critic as savvy cultural detective imbued with, to quote Amanda Anderson, "aggrandized agency." Meredith insists upon the crucial responsibility of readers to recognize the power of literature to produce and shape cultural subjects—a credo still in force in much literary scholarship—but more important, he underscores the difficulty of reading through or beyond one's own culturally produced subjectivity to achieve critical distance, a point that bears reiteration even now.

In *The Egoist* and his aesthetic manifesto, *An Essay in Comedy*, written two years earlier, Meredith develops an elaborate definition of comedy as disinterested perception with which to imagine a civilization evolving through the simultaneous refinement of its gender dynamics and aesthetic sensibilities. Comedy is the antidote to cultural stagnation and even degeneration. For Meredith, social and aesthetic refinements are routed through the "female of the species." Meredith imagines Woman in a vexed relationship to culture: that is, by dint of social constraints, she is part free agent and part object. She is, in many ways, a product in circulation on the marriage market, with limited powers of choice, hampered by social conventions, class distinctions, and economic concerns; insofar as she has agency, it is in her ability to exercise her aesthetic taste as a consumer. Meredith describes this intersected relationship in *An Essay:*

> There has been fun in Bagdad. But there never will be civilization where comedy is not possible; and that comes of some degree of social equality of the sexes. I am not quoting the Arab to exhort and disturb the somnolent East; rather for cultivated women to recognize that the comic Muse is one of their best friends. They are blind to their interests in swelling the ranks of the sentimentalists. Let them look with their clearest vision abroad and at home. They will see that, where they have no social freedom, comedy is absent; where they are household drudges, the form of comedy is primitive; where they are tolerably independent, but uncultivated, exciting melodrama takes its place, and a sentimental version of them ... But where women are on the road to an equal footing with men, in attainments and in liberty—there, and only waiting to be transplanted from life to the stage, or the novel, or the poem, pure comedy flourishes, and is, as it would help them to be, the sweetest of diversions, the wisest of delightful companions. (32)

In this conflation of Woman and Comedy both become superior products of culture, capable of being "the sweetest of diversions, the wisest of delightful companions." But Woman must also be the cultural agent who chooses Comedy over sentimental or melodramatic literature. Only through the correct aesthetic choices can social advances be made, or conversely, only through social advance may "refined" aesthetics be cultivated and appreciated.[8] As Meredith writes in the prelude to *The Egoist:* "[Comedy] it is who proposes the correcting of pretentiousness, of inflation, of dulness, and of the vestiges of rawness and grossness to be found among us. She is the ultimate civilizer, the polisher, a sweet cook" (36). The fear, however, is that Woman will not be able to choose wisely, that she will prefer the sentimental, the melodramatic, the "easy read" over the challenge of Comedy, which offers an almost-painful, if beneficial, antidote to retrograde culture.

For Meredith, then, fears about the inadequacy of Woman's aesthetic judgment extend to fears about the inadequacy of sexual selection to preserve and promote the "race." Just as in the literary marketplace Woman chooses the sentimental over "true Comedy," likewise in the marriage market she may choose according to foolish sentiments, false literary ideals. Meredith puts it this way in *An Essay:* "Is it not preferable to be the pretty idiot, the passive beauty, the adorable bundle of caprices, very feminine, very sympathetic, of romantic and sentimental fiction? Our women are taught to think so" (15). This emphasis on the productive power of fiction suggests a crucial responsibility for the cultivated reader to *be* cultivated, to be willing to eschew pleasant fictions in favor of clear-sightedness, not just for the sake of personal enlightenment, but to protect and promote the "race" itself: eugenics by way of aesthetics.

GOOD BREEDING

We must remember that progress is no invariable rule. It is most difficult to say why one civilised nation rises, becomes more powerful, and spreads more widely, than another; or why the same nation progresses more at one time than at another. We can only say that it depends on an increase in the actual number of the population, on the number of men endowed with high intellectual and moral faculties, as well as on their standard of excellence.

—Charles Darwin, *The Descent of Man* (1871)

That the appreciation of "good art" should have the power to shape the future of civilization is an idea that by no means originates with Meredith; indeed, given his insistence upon cultural refinement in both *The Egoist* and *An Essay,* arguably one might read him as "post-

Arnoldian" as much as "post-Darwinian." In Meredith's definition of Comedy as "the ultimate civilizer," one can hear distinct echoes of Arnold's famous definition of culture:

> If culture, then, is a study of perfection, and of harmonious perfection, general perfection, and perfection which consists in becoming something rather than in having something, in an inward condition of the mind and spirit, not in an outward set of circumstances,—it is clear that culture ... has a very important function to fulfill for mankind. (*Culture* 62–63)

Here Arnold advocates a kind of responsibility to the public sphere through individual, internalized consumption of culture, much as Meredith contends in *An Essay* that personal consumption of good (comic) as opposed to bad (melodramatic and sentimental) literature will save civilization.

But it is important not to imagine Darwin and Arnold as representing opposite poles of influences for Meredith. Inasmuch as Meredith's program of literary innovation is linked to his critique of scientific positivism, so too the kind of cultural analysis and critique that Arnold offers in *Culture and Anarchy* or "The Function of Criticism at the Present Time" implies a kind of evolution of humankind through the diffusion of culture, or, in Arnold's terms, "sweetness and light":

> Culture has one great passion, the passion for sweetness and light. It has one even yet greater!—the passion for making them *prevail*. It is not satisfied till we *all* come to a perfect man; it knows that the sweetness and light of the few must be imperfect until the raw and unkindled masses of humanity are touched with sweetness and light. (*Culture* 79)[9]

The deciding factor in the rise or decline of civilization—the missing link, if you will, between aesthetic production/consumption and social evolution—is the public body and its appetites, a body that, left to its own devices, represents destructive (consumptive) potential almost without limit, but bred up properly has the potential to achieve an evolved state of perfection. Within this paradigm the "few" who understand and revere culture are responsible for the husbandry of the masses, a kind of cultural "selective breeding" and management to promote "sweetness and light" among the "raw and unkindled masses."

Arnold's emphasis on "good breeding" is articulated in his dictum to "know the best that is thought and known in the world" ("Function" 37). For Arnold, this disinterested appreciation of culture will save Britain from moral and social decline. In foundational eugenicist text *Hereditary Genius,* published the same year as Arnold's *Culture and Anarchy,* Francis Galton demonstrates a strikingly similar concern with the "greatest hits" of Western civilization and a similar goal of rescuing British civilization from degeneration. In *Hereditary Genius,* he uses a complex system of grades in which he blends considerations of natural and sexual selection with assessments of cultural sophistication and mental abilities. His grading system works both within a society, as a means of judging the numbers of men who meet or approach "genius level," and without, as a means of comparing different societies by way of their total numbers of "high grade" individuals.[10]

This system can be used to circumvent the "unnatural selection" that civilization forces upon human animals. For example, Galton uses a comparison of nineteenth-century Britain with ancient Greece both to illustrate the level of cultural perfection to which Britain might aspire (if it could produce geniuses like Socrates, Plato, Aeschylus, and Sophocles) and to suggest the unhappy possibility that if the Greek civilization could crumble, so too could the British Empire. He writes:

> The average ability of the Athenian race is, on the lowest possible estimate, very nearly two grades higher than our own ... This estimate, which may seem prodigious to some, is confirmed by the quick intelligence and high culture of the Athenian commonalty, before whom literary works were recited, and works of art exhibited, of a far more severe character than could possibly be appreciated by the average of our race, the caliber of whose intellect is easily gauged by a glance at the contents of a railway bookstall. (342)

Not only do the exemplary cultural achievements of the Greeks provide a high-water mark for the Victorians, but even further, a comparison of the *consumers* of those cultural products with the "bookstall" consumers of nineteenth-century England underscores the dangers of vulgar tastes.

Galton's use of the "Athenian race" as a cautionary tale employs the same kind of aesthetic judgments as Arnold's *Culture and Anarchy,* but it ties the education of taste directly to the management (or mismanagement) of Woman's biological fertility. As he says of the ancient Greeks:

> We know, and may guess something more, of the reason why this marvelously gifted race declined. Social morality grew exceedingly lax; marriage became unfashionable, and was avoided; many of the more ambitious and accomplished women were avowed courtesans, and consequently infertile, and the mothers of the incoming population were of a heterogeneous class. (342–43)

The most highly cultivated women are precisely the ones not breeding, and the influx of mediocre and prolific "breeders" undermines the physical and cultural superiority of the civilization. In other words, there is a disconnect between the efficiency of mechanisms governing procreative breeding and the promotion of civilized ideals of "good breeding."

Galton's "hands-on" approach to managed breeding of humans may seem antithetical to Arnold's adherence to the disengaged contemplation of the "best that is known and thought in the world," but it is precisely the "multiplication" of those culturally superior specimens about which both Galton and Arnold agree. For each of these writers, the vision of a (prolific) uncultivated mass of "railway bookstall" readers offers a frightening picture of England in decline. The acquisition and promotion of culture, then, is not just about aesthetic refinement, but also about perfecting the race. Galton expresses it this way:

> The number of the races of mankind that have been entirely destroyed under the pressure of the requirements of an incoming civilization, reads us a terrible lesson … [T]he human denizens of vast regions have been entirely swept away in the short space of three centuries, less by the pressure of a stronger race than through the influence of a civilization they were incapable of supporting. And we too, the foremost labourers in creating this civilization, are beginning to show ourselves incapable of keeping pace with our own work. (344–45)

To shepherd the masses in their procreative and cultural breeding demands experts in cultivation—intellectual figures who are capable of both identifying "good" culture (i.e. the art and philosophy of ancient Greece, not the fodder of railway bookstalls) and leading and breeding the masses to appreciate that good.

CULTURAL EXPERTISE

We have scarcely done justice in our preceding remarks to the delicate charm, at once a subtly sympathetic insight and a generous truthfulness, with which Mr. Meredith has pourtrayed [sic] the best feminine types among those that come to view on the social surface ... Yet may we not hope from Mr. Meredith some day a fuller exposition of that 'perfect woman' who we are sure is no stranger to his conceptions? ... May we not trust that he who has seen so well and thrown with so bold a hand on the canvas the different lights in which the most serious problems present themselves to different minds, may, by some clear illuminating ray cast from his own in some future work, aid in the great task of social regeneration.

—Arabella Shore, "The Novels of George Meredith" (1879)

Recent critics like Amanda Anderson have suggested that Arnold's emphasis on the individual's consumption of culture places him on an intellectual trajectory with the increasingly individualized and isolated subject of aestheticism, and through aestheticism, the antisocial subject of high modernism. In this way the figure of the inward-looking and isolated aesthete offers the bridge over the "Great Divide" between the Victorian and the modern. In a chronological continuum of social interaction, the didacticism and reformative ethics of the Victorian realist social novel give way to the solipsistic introversion of the high modernist text.[11] Anderson discovers in Arnold's cultural theory "the inability to imagine reciprocal social relations as a site where one's own principles might be enacted. His protestations about the social dimensions of culture notwithstanding, Arnold seems incapable of construing social interaction in concrete terms" (118).

I want to suggest, however, that reading midcentury theories of aesthetic consumption like Arnold's against social evolutionary models of progress creates a very different trajectory: one that interprets late-Victorian literary consumption not in terms of the isolated experience of the aesthete, but in terms of the mass evolution or decline of the "race." It offers an alternative path to high modernism—one in which the ethical, social interactions that Anderson finds absent in Arnold's thinking manifest precisely within the process of cultural consumption. The "study of perfection" is not necessarily an unmediated or isolated activity but one structured by the critical discourse that precedes the moment of consumption. Arnold's famous dictum in "The Function of Criticism" is to "know the best that is known and thought in the world." But the "other half" of Arnold's charge to his readers is to transmit this knowledge and thus "to create a current of true and fresh ideas" (37). In other words, the ideals of culture are transmitted in the concrete form of cultural objects. And the interaction of individual with individual in the social realm may be asynchronous, but it is nonetheless powerfully engaged, engaging, and transformative. Viewed this way, literature, rather than being increasingly abstracted from the public realm and the marketplace, consolidates a pivotal ethical position in both, and the literary critic reaches for a new prominence as the "reader" of a civilization's future—a prophet.

Meredith places himself, like Arnold, as an "expert" at the vanguard of culture, in a position to husband his readers. In his role as "cultural expert," Meredith's expertise is based on an understanding not only of aesthetics but also of evolutionary science and, more important, of the interconnections between the two. The authority that Meredith claims is just that "prophet in the wilderness" stance that Arnold adopts in *Culture and Anarchy* when he cautions that "culture has a rough task to achieve in this country. Its preachers have, and are likely long to have, a hard time of it" (63). It is via this outsider persona that Meredith represents the work the novelist should do. As he writes in the opening chapter of *Diana of the Crossways*:

> Dozens of writers will be in at yonder yawning breach, if only perusers will rally to the philosophic standard. They are sick of the woodeny puppetry they dispense ... Well, if not dozens, half-dozens; gallant pens are alive; one can speak of them in the plural. I venture to say that they would be satisfied with a dozen for an audience, for a commencement ... But the example is the thing; sacrifices must be expected. The example might, one hopes, create a taste. (15)

By claiming a position in the unpopular minority, the cultural expert places himself in the position of writing to readers who don't exist yet, or at least don't exist in any great numbers. And he imagines both enlightened readers and writers as willing to sacrifice for a good cause.

It is a neatly circular self-authorization: the mass of readers lacks the cultural acumen to appreciate the lessons that an expert like Arnold or Meredith has to offer, and that is precisely why the expert must continue, lonely and misunderstood, to do the work of Culture, for the good of those very unappreciative masses who don't see any need for the work. And eventually society will evolve, through the influence of Culture, to value and foster Culture. Arnold, for instance, proclaims in "The Function of Criticism": "The mass of mankind will never have any ardent zeal for seeing things as they are … That is as much as saying that whoever sets himself to see things as they are will find himself one of a very small circle; but it is only by this small circle doing its own work that adequate ideas will ever get current at all" (41).

It is important to recognize that this is, first and foremost, a rhetorical stance. Whatever may be the demographics of *actual* readership, the implied audience of the cultural expert is not the uncultivated reader who will flip past the turgid opening chapters to look for the first good love scene or melodramatic cliff-hanger. Rather, it is the fellow "apostle of culture" whose appreciation of the turgid but meaningful prose signifies his or her membership in the "very small circle" of true believers. For example, Arnold describes the nearly universal excoriation of the "lovers of culture" in England, but he refers to those lovers with a cozily inclusive "we." And as Virginia Woolf writes: "Meredith pays us a supreme compliment to which as novel-readers we are little accustomed. We are civilized people, he seems to say, watching the comedy of human relations together. Human relations are of profound interest … He imagines us capable of disinterested curiosity in the behaviour of our kind. This is so rare a compliment from a novelist to his reader that we are at first bewildered and then delighted" ("Novels" 230). Meredith's "difficulties," Woolf argues, must be understood in evolutionary terms: he is an innovator, responsible for "mutations" in the genre of the novel. As mutations, these may sometimes be unlovely, but as she points out:

> When [Meredith] wrote, in the seventies and eighties of the last century, the novel had reached a stage where it could only exist by moving onward … George Eliot, Meredith, and Hardy were all imperfect novelists largely because they insisted upon introducing qualities, of thought and of poetry, that are perhaps incompatible with fiction at its most perfect. On the other hand, if fiction had remained what it was to Jane Austen and Trollope, fiction would by this time be dead … To read Meredith, then, to our greatest advantage we must make certain allowances and relax certain standards. We must not expect the perfect quietude of a traditional style nor the triumphs of a patient and pedestrian psychology. (230–31)

In other words, if Meredith's work were enjoyable, it would only be rehearsing the form and tropes of "dead" fiction; its unpleasantness is a mark of its advanced status, and insofar as one chooses to read Meredith (and make allowances), this too is a mark of the reader's advanced status. This rhetorical insistence on including the reader has the very important effects of emphasizing the ethics of reading and of demanding the reader's responsibility. For it is not simply reading, but breeding that is at work.

Thus, in 1892 (the time during which Woolf claims Meredith's popularity was at its height) literary critic W. J. Dawson asserts:

> Meredith is a fruitful force, working not directly but indirectly on the mass of readers, not in his own person so much as in a far wider degree through the persons of others who have received the impact of his teaching. It is perhaps not as we could wish it, and not as he could wish it. But if it be for the present a thing inevitable there is this compensation, that as the race progresses he will become more and more visible in the general life. (170–71)

In other words, to judge by Meredith critics and scholars, there is no time at which George Meredith has been understood or properly appreciated by "the masses," and yet there seems always to have been a "mass" of critics working as Meredith apologists—present critic included even—who must explain and defend his cultural worth. Indeed, as a reviewer for the *Saturday Review* writes of *The Egoist:* "Those who persevere to the end of the book will find their reward. They have been fairly warned that there will be some hard reading to accomplish. There must be no skipping; the book must be read, not page by page like the ordinary novel, but line by line" (222). And C. Monkhouse in his 1885 review describes the experience of reading *Diana of the Crossways* thus:

> What [Meredith] calls the "literary covering" of his ideas makes his books hard reading even to the hard-headed, and the swiftness and agility of his thought requires more intellectual exercise than most readers are able or willing to take. Those who take it will be rewarded not only mentally, but morally. (264)[12]

One might argue that these critics offer the proof that Meredith was a fruitful force, for their discussions of his work sound much like Meredith's own theories of reading, literature, and culture. As Archibald Henderson claims, with "Meredithian" imagery in

Interpreters of Life and the Modern Spirit (1911): "The educative influence of his fictive achievement, so arabesque, so fantastically kaleidoscopic, so ravishingly tortuous, yet withal so clear-visioned, so intense and so hardly sane, has been imperceptibly if glacially slow and sure" (5).

What is more or less explicit in all these accounts is that working hard at novel-reading is a mark of the reader's participation in the advance of culture. Whereas Woolf's image of the "perfect but dead" novels of Trollope and Austen grants to Meredith the role of evolutionary mutation (an imperfect but necessary leap forward), Dawson's discussion of the influence of his work is both explicitly Arnoldian in the picture of an almost-mystical diffusion of ideas and in its criticism of the "philistine mediocrity" that doesn't appreciate Meredith, and also evolutionary in its language of racial progress. In accusing Meredith's critics of "intellectual indolence," Dawson accuses them implicitly of arresting the development of civilization:

> To such people ... poetry and fiction are simply ingenious relaxations for the idle moments of life, of which they have too many, and they naturally demand the old commonplaces of pursuing love and ultimate marriage bells as the beginning and end of fiction, and resent a style of fiction which is charged with the gravest matter and is meant to make men think. (167)

Clearly Dawson's assumption of a gendered demographic of the readership of "commonplace" fiction—in that readers with too much idle time upon their hands, enjoying the sentimental stories about love and "ultimate marriage bells" are contrasted with those vigorous intellectual readers who choose that matter which "is meant to make men think"—rehearses a well-known Victorian (and modernist) denigration of the popular, mass-market, and sentimental feminine as opposed to the innovative, intellectual, and antiestablishment masculine. This dichotomy, however, is one that is both reinforced and problematized in Meredith's discussion of Comedy. Although Meredith certainly decries the sentimental female reader, he also explores the possibility, indeed necessity, of her education; consequently, the opposition lies not between the female mass-market consumer and male cultural expert, per se, but between the uneducated female consumer and the possibility of her evolution to culturally expert consumer.

THE EGOIST: "CAPTIVATING PASSAGES ...
IN A STYLE NOT UNFAMILIAR"

*Total ignorance being their pledge of purity to men, [women] have to expunge the
writing of their perceptives on the tablets of their brain: they have to know not when
they do know ... Wonder in no degree that they indulge a craving to be fools, or that
many of them act the character ... You have reared them to this pitch, and at this pitch
they have partly civilized you.*

—George Meredith, *The Egoist* (1879)

Meredith's mixed metaphor shows that women are simultaneously
the consumers of texts and the texts themselves that are produced
for and consumed by men in the marriage market who will then
be civilized (at least imperfectly) by the women they consume. You
may judge a civilization by the women that it rea(r/d)s. And what
if the female reader clings to the "old commonplaces" of romance
plots and marriage resolutions? Then she participates in her own
enslavement and relegates herself and, by extension, her culture to a
retrograde, uncultivated state. As the narrator tells us in *The Egoist*:

> The capaciously strong in soul among women will ultimately detect
> an infinite grossness in the demand for purity infinite, spotless
> bloom. Earlier or later they see they have been victims of the singu-
> lar Egoist, have worn the mask of ignorance to be named innocent,
> have turned themselves into market produce for his delight, and
> have really abandoned the commodity in ministering to the lust for
> it ... Are they not of nature warriors, like men?—men's mates to bear
> them heroes instead of puppets? But the devouring male Egoist pre-
> fers them as inanimate overwrought polished pure metal precious
> vessels, fresh from the hands of the artificer, for him to walk away
> with hugging, call his own, drink of, and fill, and drink of, and forget
> that he stole them. (152)

The image that Meredith offers here of the "devouring male Egoist,"
demanding his women as "spotless" commodities on the market,
points precisely to the aesthetic-evolutionary problem of Woman
in culture: if woman is to be the cultural artifact, the "inanimate
overwrought polished pure metal precious vessel," then she cannot
also be a "warrior."

This would seem to suggest that agency is an either-or propo-
sition (warriors have it; vessels don't), but for Meredith it's more

complicated than that, for if Woman is the overwrought vessel, she is also the "artificer." She creates, and worse, consumes her own sentimentalized image. In other words, not only must she package herself for the market, but she must also buy what she is selling. According to Meredith's narrator: "[Young women] are trained to please man's taste, for which purpose they soon learn to live out of themselves, and look on themselves as he looks, almost as little disturbed as he by the undiscovered" (302). The work of femininity in this complex scenario is the work of "undiscovery," of the violent subduing of knowledge in exchange for self-objectification, with the consolatory, sentimental illusions of "the old commonplaces of pursuing love and ... marriage bells" (Dawson 167).

From the vantage point of the cultural expert, the picture of women "indulg[ing] a craving to be fools" offers the most disturbing vision of the novel. This indulgence places the heroine, Clara Middleton, in the initial quandary—her betrothal to the morally repugnant Sir Willoughby—and it continues to thwart her efforts to free herself through the very end of the novel. The overwhelming questions that the novel seems to ask are these: How "free" is Clara, not just to make choices, but to make the *right* choices? How much is she hindered by the conventions of her social realm, not just in acting on her desires, but in desiring wisely? And, finally, how much is Clara hindered by what hinders the readers of her story: the conventions of the novel genre itself, which demand of its heroines that they marry and live happily ever after?

As has been ably discussed in previous analyses of *The Egoist*, the conflicts of the plot are represented in evolutionary terms. The parasitic Sir Willoughby imagines that Clara's choice of him among suitors confirms the success of sexual selection and, therefore, his own superiority: "She cannot help herself; it is her nature, and her nature is the guarantee for the noblest race of men to come of her ... Science thus—or it is better to say—an acquaintance with science facilitates the cultivation of aristocracy" (72).[13] Clara, regretting her choice of Willoughby, spends the bulk of the novel railing against her imprisonment and falling in love with Willoughby's poor but physically and intellectually vigorous cousin, Vernon Whitford. The novel ends, happily, with Clara's escape from Willoughby into Vernon's open arms and with Willoughby's winning, as a consolation prize, the hand of Laetitia Dale, a faded and sickly beauty who will marry him only for money, and who will not be strong enough to produce children. Thus, disaster is narrowly averted: the healthy breeders will breed, and the effete and jaded will be removed from the genetic stock. This resolves the problems of the plot on a basic biological evolutionary level. But if one reads Meredith as not just post-Darwinian, but as post-Arnoldian as well, the resolution creates other problems for the more-complicated issues of cultural education and social evolution.

As Clara realizes, the female prerogative of choice is circumscribed, at best, by woman's inadequate upbringing:

> It must be an ill-constructed tumbling world where the hour of ignorance is made the creator of our destiny by being forced to the decisive elections upon which life's main issues hang ... Without imputing blame to [Willoughby], for she was reasonable so far, she deemed herself a person entrapped. In a dream somehow she had committed herself to a life-long imprisonment. (133)

Clara is clear-sighted enough to understand that she has been led, by her ignorance and youth and susceptibility to romance, to attach herself to a man at once ridiculous and, by virtue of his absolute control over her, sinister. Nevertheless, she is not quite clear-sighted or strong enough to extricate herself; she is still ignorant, young, and susceptible to sentimental and melodramatic fantasies.

As a result, although one might place the conflict of the novel in the battle between Willoughby and Clara (he to hold on to her, and she to escape from him), one might also read it in Clara's vacillation between the "woman warrior" she might be in an ideal world and the weak, sentimental woman that she has been taught to be. In the same way, the novel constantly blurs the difference between what one reads and what one is. It offers a series of passages in which the reader may read reading, or to put it another way, the novel presents a series of situations in which the choice between blind sentiment and clear-sighted Comedy is offered not only to the characters but also to the reader. This is a dynamic that *The Egoist* illustrates playfully; at the end of a description of Willoughby's obtuse misreading of Clara's physical aversion to him (which he interprets as feminine coyness), the narrator remarks: "And if you ask whether a man, sensitive and a lover, can be so blinded, you are condemned to reperuse the foregoing paragraph" (152). The throwaway one-liner seems to poke fun both at the reader who might miss the point and at the labyrinthine prose, the rereading of which is a punishment to be dreaded. The joke that Meredith shares with his reader here is one that is less obvious elsewhere when, perhaps, the reader's sympathies are more firmly engaged with less risible characters. I want to focus particularly on the instances when *The Egoist* simultaneously represents, encourages, and derides the "uncultivated" cravings for sentimental melodrama.

When, for instance, faced with the possibility of losing Clara, Willoughby comforts himself with a fantasy of her lifelong repentance and a tearful, bittersweet reunion, he is both ludicrous and malevolent—clearly not an attractive character to inspire imitation:

> Supposing her still youngish, there might be captivating passages between them, as thus, in a style not unfamiliar:
> "And was it my fault, my poor girl? Am I to blame, that you have passed a lonely, unloved youth?"
> "No, Willoughby! The irreparable error was mine, the blame is mine, mine only. I live to repent it. I do not seek, for I have not deserved, your pardon. Had I it, I should need my own self-esteem to presume to clasp it to a bosom ever unworthy of you."
> "... Clara! one—one only—one last—one holy kiss!"
> "If these poor lips, that once were sweet to you ..."
> The kiss, to continue the language of the imaginative composition of his time, favourite readings in which had inspired Sir Willoughby with a colloquy so pathetic, was imprinted.
> Ay, she had the kiss, and no mean one. It was intended to swallow every vestige of dwindling attractiveness out of her, and there was a bit of scandal springing of it in the background that satisfactorily settled her business. (278–79)

Willoughby's blithe combination of "pathetic colloquy" and vampiric sadism, in addition to highlighting his desire for revenge, does a couple of things: First, it borrows wholesale from that melodramatic touchstone, Mrs. Henry Wood's *East Lynne.* Consider the tear-jerking deathbed scene between the fallen Isabel Vane and her stern but forgiving ex-husband:

> "Do you remember ... my promising to be your wife?—and the first kiss you left upon my lips?—and oh, Archibald! do you remember how happy we were with each other? ... "
> Ay. He did remember it. He took that poor hand into his, retaining there its wasted fingers.
> "Had you any reproach to cast to me?" he gently said, bending his head a little.

"Reproach to you! To you who must be almost without reproach in the sight of Heaven! you, who were ever loving to me, ever anxious for my welfare! When I think of what you were, and are, and how I requited you, I could sink into the earth with remorse and shame." (627)

Second, in borrowing from *East Lynne*, *The Egoist* suggests that the pleasure of melodrama lies in the reader's feeding off the spectacular suffering of the heroine.[14] In light of Meredith's explicit linking of melodrama with the uncultivated civilization, Willoughby's "favourite readings" must register as one of his more-serious flaws—indeed, inseparable from his subjugation of his women. The fiction consumed by Willoughby is, in fact, a fantasy *of* consumption, of "swallowing" the attractive female. For the female reader, then, to indulge in such fictions is to consume herself.

Yet this is precisely what Clara does when she constructs her own bittersweet reunion fantasy about a meeting with Vernon; she both creates and consumes a similarly "fictional" scenario:

What would he think? They might never meet, for her to know. Or one day in the Alps they might meet, a middle-aged couple, he famous, she regretful only to have fallen below his lofty standard. "For, Mr Whitford," says she, very earnestly, "I did wish at that time, believe me or not, to merit your approbation." The brows of the phantom Vernon whom she conjured up were stern, as she had seen them yesterday in the library. (302–3)

Clara's desperate desire for a rescuer to carry her away from Willoughby (as his previous fiancée, Constantia Durham, was carried away by Harry Oxford) produces various scenarios throughout the novel in which Clara tries to fit Vernon into the role of romantic hero: "'If I were loved! ... If some noble gentleman could see me as I am and not disdain to aid me! Oh! to be caught up out of this prison of thorns and brambles. I cannot tear my own way out. I am a coward'" (141). Although Clara's weakness in indulging the fantasy is clear, it is also clear that her circumstances provide little scope for imagination otherwise. In her semicultivated state, melodrama is the genre of choice.

But what of the reader's aesthetic choices? When *we* read voraciously for the development of Vernon and Clara's forbidden love—thrill to Vernon's stoical suffering of his secret attraction to Clara, feel Clara's frustrated longing for his approval—is not the novel providing the very *East Lynne*-ish melodrama and sentimentality that it decries? We too, then, have bought into the sentimentality and romance of the domestic plot, and the violence that it both masks and perpetuates. [15] *The Egoist* offers the reader the resolution of Clara and Vernon's impending marriage. But the genre of the melodrama demands a female sacrifice: some woman must be swallowed up. In purchasing Clara's freedom from marriage to Willoughby, the novel sells Laetitia into that very bondage. To read Laetitia's fate and still be pleased with our happy ending means that we must forget our own clarity of vision and engage in our very own version of "knowing not when we do know," a disavowal that Clara herself performs at the end of the novel. When Clara has been freed from her engagement, she suddenly cannot understand how Laetitia could possibly resist Willoughby's entreaties:

> "Dear, dear friend," said Clara. "Why—I presume on your tenderness for me; but let me: to-morrow I go—why will you reject your happiness? … Can it be that you have any doubt of the strength of this attachment? I have none. I have never had a doubt that it was the strongest of his feelings … If I might know this was to be, which all desire, before I leave, I should not feel as I do now. I long to see you happy … him, yes, him too. Is it like asking you to pay my debt? Then, please! But, no; I am not more than partly selfish on this occasion. He has won my gratitude." (579)

Even Clara, who should know better than anyone Willoughby's repulsive character—who even acknowledges the grim reality that Laetitia will pay her debt in marrying Willoughby—refuses to understand Laetitia's objections and joins in the chorus of people attempting to persuade her to accept him.

Critics have tended to read Laetitia in terms of what she will mean to Willoughby as his wife, rather than as one who will enter into the marriage with her own thoughts and feelings. Even Patricia O'Hara, who concedes that Laetitia's fate is "more than a little disturbing," ends her analysis of the novel with this sanguine comment: "And as things turn out, nature has not selected Willoughby after all: Laetitia Dale's faded health dims the prospect of Patterne heirs and increases the probability of the extinction of the line" (18–19). And Gillian

Beer, who astutely describes Laetitia's psychological complexity, comes to the following conclusion: "When Laetitia at last declares her changed feelings for Willoughby, we can greet the stroke ... with delighted recognition" (*Meredith* 127). Richard Stevenson builds the entire argument of his article "Laetitia Dale and the Comic Spirit in *The Egoist*" around the premise that "there is nothing tragic or even pathetic about Laetitia's marriage to Willoughby" (406).[16]

Yet it is hard to imagine feeling a sense of "delighted recognition" in Laetitia's final resistance to Willoughby:

> "You will not detain me here, Sir Willoughby?"
>
> "I will detain you. I will use force and guile. I will spare nothing."
>
> ... "But do you know what you ask for? Do you remember what I told you of myself? I am hard, materialistic; I have lost faith in romance, the skeleton is present with me all over my life. And my health is not good. I crave for money. I should marry to be rich. I should not worship you. I should be a burden, a barely living one, irresponsive and cold. Conceive of such a wife, Sir Willoughby!"
>
> "It will be you!"
>
> She tried to recall how this would have sung in her ears long back. Her bosom rose and fell in absolute dejection. Her ammunition of arguments against him had been expended overnight. (593–94)

If, like Clara, readers are willing to pass over Laetitia's fate, then they (we) are doing precisely what Meredith describes: choosing to "know not when they do know."

Therefore, while *The Egoist* stresses the importance of reading rightly—comically and with a clear vision, and not sentimentally—it does not necessarily encourage that right kind of reading. In many ways the novel is not, as its subtitle says, "a Comedy in Narrative" so much as it is a "Comedy in Interpretation." For if "Comedy" is the refined, disinterested lens through which to view the foibles of society and self, it is also the generic structure that depends on a sentimental attachment to romance and that demands marriage as its happy resolution. By forcing the reader's complicity with the latter even as it preaches adherence to the former, the novel provides a complexly layered and uncomfortable critique of the role of novels and novel-reading in the progression or regression of civilization.

THE FUNCTION OF COMEDY AT THE PRESENT TIME

[The comic idea] is not provoked in the order of nature, until we draw its penetrating attentiveness to some circumstance with which we have been mixing our private interests, or our speculative obfuscation.

　　—George Meredith, *An Essay on Comedy* (1877)

For Meredith, the kind of critical reading we do has the potential to rescue or imperil civilization. However, one crucial dimension of Meredith's literary theory—the significant responsibility of the reader—often seems to drop out of critical discussions of his work. Critics of *The Egoist* have certainly noted Meredith's feminist sympathies, as they have his Darwinian leanings, and his experimentation with form. Likewise, they have observed that the controlling vision of *The Egoist* is an ironic one; they have pointed to the ironies of the civilized savagery of masculine sexual appetites, of the distance between the sentimental language of courtship and the brutal realities of the marriage market, of the imbedded meaning in Willoughby Patterne's name, and of the use of the tropes of Restoration comedy in a "progressive" novel. Various critics have attempted to situate the ironic vision of the novel with one character or another. Richard Stevenson asserts that "[Laetitia's] point of view is a primary means by which Meredith manages to keep our critical responses to Willoughby under control" (407). Conversely, Carolyn Williams argues that

> through the narrator/Clara, we learn the proper ironic perspective on Willoughby … we learn to regard her confusion as an indication of the ironic distance between what Willoughby seems and what he means. This gap between Willoughby's appearance and his reality, into which Clara falls as if it were a bottomless abyss, is the space of irony into which we fall with pleasure. (63)

And Gary Handwerk maintains that the novel's "irony exists as a hermeneutic and intersubjective phenomenon embodied in a particular mode of interaction, linguistic though not necessarily conscious, between subjects" (166). These readings offer persuasive accounts of the intricate exchanges and nuances through which the novel creates an edifying picture of the Egoist, but they miss the point that Meredith is at pains to underscore from the very first chapter of the novel: in our "infinitesimal" reading of the "Book" we are in danger of losing sight of our own countenances.

In following the intricacies of Meredith's comic plot, character development, or language, it is possible to miss a layer of his irony, falling into the same traps as the Egoist himself—that is, relying on a complacent distance between the object of critique and the ironically detached "I" of the observer. Gillian Beer, for example, asserts, "This detachment and control is of the essence of comedy, and Meredith sustains it almost throughout *The Egoist*." Where ironic distance fails in the novel, Beer argues, is where Meredith diverges from his idea of comedy, so carefully articulated in *An Essay* ("Idea of Comedy" 167). If, according to Beer, Meredith's "detachment and control" signals his use of Comedy, then the critical position from which Beer can claim that Meredith has "almost" sustained the artistic aim he set out to accomplish signals her own "detachment and control" over the text. As she writes: "If the reader's role is to be primarily that of judge, it is necessary that our detachment should be sustained" (*Meredith* 130).

Yet in *An Essay* Meredith eschews this critical distance. He says of Comedy: "You may estimate your capacity for comic perception by being able to detect the ridicule of them you love without loving them the less; and more by being able to see yourself somewhat ridiculous in dear eyes, and accepting the correction their image of you proposes" (42). In other words, comedy is *not* about "detachment and control," but rather about acknowledging one's complicity in the ridiculous, the fallible, and the correctable.[17] This is an uncomfortable position, as Meredith acknowledges in his discussion of the failings of a cultivated and observant, but uncomic, middle-class readership:

> Humorous writing they will endure, perhaps approve, if it mingles with pathos to shake and elevate the feelings. They approve of satire, because, like the beak of a vulture, it smells of carrion, which they are not. But of comedy they have a shivering dread, for comedy enfolds them with the wretched host of the world, huddles them with us all in an ignoble assimilation, and cannot be used by any exalted variety as a scourge and a broom. Nay, to be an exalted variety is to come under the calm, curious eye of the Comic Spirit, and be probed for what you are. (13–14)

Comedy is precisely where ironic distance is *not* wholly possible, where critical objectivity must be suspect because we have been "mixing our private interests" with the object of study.

In its suspicion of the reader's investments, the novel echoes Matthew Arnold's disdain for a "polemical practical criticism [that] makes men blind even to the ideal imperfection of their practice" ("Function" 38). Like Arnold, Meredith questions the will to interpret, to inflict a particular reading on a text in order to get the satisfaction of a resolution, a lesson, a cure. *The Egoist*'s narrator, for instance, remarks:

> Observers of a gathering complication and a character in action commonly resemble gleaners who are intent only on picking up the ears of grain and huddling their store. Disinterestedly or interestedly they wax over-eager for the little trifles, and make too much of them … And they may be accurate observers without being good judges. They do not think so, and their bent is to glean hurriedly and form conclusions as hasty, when their business should be to sift at each step, and question. (288)

As a "turgid" narrative aside that freezes the plot, this passage offers a good example of the novel's Arnoldian ethos and its trickiness. It asks for abstract contemplation at a moment when the plot is moving forward with a "gathering complication," and an inattentive or uncultivated reader might be tempted to rush ahead to the fulfillment of plot expectations. The passage comes when Vernon and Laetitia, watching Clara interact with the rakish Horace McCray, both assume that she is in love with Horace and will elope with him. Of course they are wrong, as the reader, with the help of the narrator's commentary, can see. The love story that seems self-evident to Vernon and Laetitia is no more than "the rapid advance to a familiarity, more ostensible than actual, of two lively natures" (289). But Vernon and Laetitia's emotional involvement with Clara prevents accurate analysis. Supposing, however, the reader were to apply the narrator's lesson to his/her own investment in the novel, there is very little difference between the two observers' knowledge of Clara's intimacies with Horace and the reader's knowledge of Clara's intimacy with Vernon. The information we are given about her budding romance with Vernon is not much more than the "little trifles" from which Vernon and Laetitia construct a narrative about Clara and Horace, but sifting and questioning are precisely what the novel's very structure thwarts.

It is, Meredith suggests, in the nature of readers—desirous of happy endings or at least resolutions—to acquiesce, even collaborate, in their hoodwinking. But in Comedy Meredith offers a new way of reading the world: "For verily ... we must read of [the Book of Egoism] what we can of it, at least the page before us, if we would be men ... The remedy of your frightful affliction is here, through the stillatory of Comedy" (35). Moreover, this new remedy is the responsibility of the cultural critic:

> The chief consideration for us is, what particular practice of Art in letters is the best for the perusal of the Book of our common wisdom; so that with clearer minds and livelier manners we may escape, as it were, into daylight and song from a land of fog-horns. Shall we read it by the watchmaker's eye in luminous rings eruptive of the infinitesimal, or pointed with examples and types under the broad Alpine survey of the spirit born of our united social intelligence, which is the Comic Spirit? Wise men say the latter. They tell us that there is a constant tendency in the Book to accumulate excess of substance, and such repleteness, obscuring the glass it holds to mankind, renders us inexact in the recognition of our individual countenances; a perilous thing for civilization. (34–35)

In his blending of the panoramic view with "individual countenances," Meredith presents a picture of the individual as part of a larger social aggregate, as part of the "spirit born of our united social intelligence," and, as such, an individual owing a responsibility to that aggregate: to advance civilization through his or her personal reflection.

In addition, he implies a moral failing in the generic tradition of realism, because it is the accumulation of detail, ostensibly with scientific detachment but in fact governed by the sentimental demands of the genre, that continues to obscure vision and impede development toward "perfection." The work of the reader/critic in reading *The Egoist*, then, is not merely the work of interpretation, of analyzing the text, but also the work of contemplating the effects of reading the text. In other words, reading *The Egoist* is the labor of being cultivated to become the kind of reader that the novel requires: clear-sighted, compassionate, flawed perhaps (with a predilection for bad sentimental fiction, say), but striving for the "perfection which consists in becoming something." In many ways, *Diana of the Crossways* seems to represent the triumph of Meredith's cultivation of Comedy as civilizing process, yet as I will argue, Meredith's novel of 1885 extends the earlier critique of reading in *The Egoist* to offer a troubling reevaluation of the enlightened woman reader.

DIANA OF THE CROSSWAYS: "IT IS A TEST
OF THE CIVILIZED"

But she would have us away with sentimentalism. Sentimental people, in her phrase, "fiddle harmonics on the strings of sensualism," to the delight of a world gaping for marvels of musical execution rather than for music. For our world is all but a sensational world at present, in maternal travail of a soberer, a braver, a brighter-eyed. Her reflections are thus to be interpreted, it seems to me.

—George Meredith, *Diana of the Crossways* (1885)

Excitement and sensationalism of the best there are, surely, for those to whom such sensations are a necessity in their reading: in the ride of Redworth through the burning sunset "with junipers behind him"; the curious sensation stealing over his frame when he fancies he sees two figures vanishing through the churchyard, where in the moonlight the gravestones are legible ... the nightwatch of Diana, so well drawn that it is not over-drawn; and the thrilling scenes between the passionate lovers.

—Review of *Diana of the Crossways*, *Illustrated London News* (1885)

The opening chapter of *Diana of the Crossways* begins with a series of layered interpretations of Diana Warwick by the Diarists, who recount her wit and beauty and her alleged indiscretions, and by the narrator, who assesses the Diarists and through them Diana. Thus, in the quote above, we have a bon mot that the narrator reports a Diarist reporting. Diana is reputed to have said that "sentimental people ... 'fiddle harmonics on the strings of sensualism,'" but the quotation marks shed doubt on how much of the statement is hers. And then this comment is elaborated on as if by Diana herself, although we learn at the end of the explication that this interpretation too is suspect: "Her reflections are thus to be interpreted, *it seems to me.*" It is here in the "it seems to me" that Meredith offers his toughest challenge to his readers.

Clearly, this preface provides Meredith with a platform from which to promote his theory of the art of fiction. Just as he espouses Comedy in *An Essay* and *The Egoist*, here he offers Philosophy as the bringer of a better world. When we have abandoned our attachments to sensationalism—whether it is conveyed in the sentimental or grossly clinical—in favor of Philosophy,

then, ah! then, moreover, will the novelist's Art, now neither blushless infant nor executive man, have attained its majority. We can then

be veraciously historical, honestly transcriptive ... Philosophy bids
us to see that we are neither so pretty as rose-pink, not so repulsive as
dirty drab ... Do but perceive that we are coming to philosophy, the
stride toward it will be a giant's—a century in a day. And imagine the
celestial refreshment of having a pure decency in the place of sham;
real flesh; a soul born active, wind-beaten, but ascending. Honourable will fiction then appear; honourable, a fount of life, an aid to life,
quick with our blood. (13)

It would make sense, then, if *Diana* itself embodied neither the "rose-
pink" of sentiment nor the "dirty drab" of naturalism, but Meredith's
own vision of the "New Fiction," conveying our real selves to ourselves as "wholesome, bearable, fructifying, finally a delight" (13).
Indeed, while the novel does strive for this aesthetic and moral ideal,
it also tells the story of its own striving for an ideal with which the
"sensational world" is still pregnant.

Diana tells the story of a woman more advanced than *The Egoist*'s
Clara Middleton. In many ways Diana represents the "woman warrior" that *The Egoist* only imagines to be possible. She has attained,
certainly, a higher level of civilization than "the pretty idiot, the
passive beauty, the adorable bundle of caprices" that Meredith
associates with "romantic and sentimental fiction" (*An Essay* 15).
The novel rehearses many of the same problems that *The Egoist* considers: gender inequality, women's limited choices on the marriage
market, the cultural preference for falsely sentimentalized versions
of women over real, powerful, and free women. But Diana is more
forceful, more independent, more experienced, wittier, and more
passionate than Clara. Her objections to marriage are more emphatic
and prolonged, and her relationships with men more materially and
psychologically damaging. Her plight is more extreme, and so are
her attempts to free herself. As Beer notes, Diana is Meredith's "full-
est attempt at psychological realism" (*Meredith* 144).[18]

If the novel's social critique exceeds *The Egoist*'s, so too do its
sensational and romantic appeals. The scenes described in the
Illustrated London News review quoted above are indeed emotionally
fraught, even suspenseful, and if some of them reproduce scenes in
The Egoist, they do so with more "bang for the buck." For example,
in *The Egoist*, when Clara attempts to run away from Willoughby
and Patterne Hall, she walks a couple of miles in the rain to the
train station, where she is apprehended by Vernon Whitford, who
has followed her on foot and who suspects she may be eloping with

Horace De Craye (and although Clara in fact has no intention of doing so, De Craye hopes and suspects the same thing). Vernon's rescue of Clara is not without sensational appeal.[19] But although Clara's temporary escape causes a miniscandal at the hall, and although Horace De Craye attempts to seduce Clara into confiding in him after Vernon has left her to her "free will," the danger to her, if it really ever existed, is averted without much to-do; she resists De Craye's charms and returns to Patterne Hall with her virtue and reputation intact. By comparison, in *Diana of the Crossways* Diana is trapped in a marriage, not merely a betrothal, to a terrible Egoist. She makes two ill-considered attempts to escape her marriage and is rescued from her folly both times by Thomas Redworth. The first instance: after her husband has filed for divorce, Diana plans to leave the country without fighting the charges (thereby buying her freedom from Warwick at the cost of her reputation), and Redworth, entrusted with a letter from Emma Dunstane, rides at breakneck speed through the night to the Crossways to intercept her. And the second: when Diana plans to elope with Percy Dacier, Redworth again arrives fortuitously, minutes before she is to meet Dacier, to tell her that Emma is undergoing life-threatening surgery and that "you must come with me at once!" (241). In both scenes Redworth appears as a kind of cavalier, in the first delivering Emma's letter as a sacred trust, and in the second delivering Diana herself to Emma's bedside. He is thus laden not only with his own emotional freight— his loyalty, chivalry, and unrequited love for Diana—but also with Emma's passion for her friend.[20]

In addition, *Diana* offers a much more-sensational resolution to its romance than *The Egoist*. When Clara is freed from her engagement with Willoughby, the novel hands her off to Vernon in the same breath, as it were, although it delays their "official" engagement until they are away from Willoughby's house, suspending any consummation of their love, beyond the coy:

> "Vernon, no! not in this house!"
>
> That supplication coupled with his name confessed the end to which her quick vision perceived she was being led, where she would succumb.
>
> She revived the same shrinking in him from a breath of their great word yet: not here; somewhere in the shadow of the mountains.
>
> But he was sure of her. And their hands might join. The two hands thought so, or did not think, behaved like innocents. (586–87)

Conversely, when Diana is freed from her marriage by Augustus Warwick's death, and is finally free to marry Thomas Redworth, we are treated to a passionate embrace, the strength of which takes Diana herself by surprise:

> A really big storm-wave caught her from the shore and whirled her to mid-sea, out of every sensibility but the swimming one of her loss of self in the man.
> ... She was up at his heart, fast-locked, undergoing a change greater than the sea works; her thoughts one blush, her brain a fire-fount. This was not like being seated on a throne.
> "There," said he, loosening his hug, "now you belong to me! I know you from head to foot. After that, my darling, I could leave you for years, and call you wife, and be sure of you." (406)

The elliptical satisfactions of *The Egoist*'s romance are thoroughly embodied in *Diana of the Crossways*.

But if Laetitia Dale's fate dampens the comic ending of the former novel, Diana's resistance to marriage should also make the reader pause in regard to the happy resolution of the latter. Diana resists Redworth and the idea of marriage vehemently for six of the last seven chapters of the novel. The narrator describes her as

> the woman of a long widowhood, that had become a trebly sensi-tive maidenhood; abashed by her knowledge of the world, animated by her abounding blood; cherishing her new freedom, dreading the menacer; feeling, that though she held the citadel, she was daily less sure of its foundations, and that her hope of some last romance in life was going; for in him shone not a glimpse. He appeared to Diana as a fatal power, attracting her without sympathy, benevolently over-coming. (381)

Here the "romance" between Redworth and Diana is explicitly deromanticized, but this is a complicated move by the novel. Diana resists Redworth in part because he is not romantic enough to her: he is not an ideal lover, but "one of those good men, strong men, who subdue and do not kindle" (381). The narrator notes with gentle sarcasm: "The woman who talked of the sentimentalist's 'fiddling harmonics,' herself stressed the material chords, in her attempt to escape out of herself and away from her pursuer" (381). But when Diana finally succumbs, she acknowledges "her subserviency to touch and pressure—and more, stranger, her readiness to kindle" (409). How are we to read this resolution? The novel offers several possible readings.

In a way it might make sense to read it like Trollope's *Can You Forgive Her?* and *Miss Mackenzie*, in which the reluctant heroine must be brought to admit that she is not fit to pilot her own ship. Indeed, *Diana* offers an exchange between Emma and Diana that borrows the same nautical language:

> "But marriage, dear Emmy! marriage! Is marriage to be the end of me?"
>
> "What amazing apotheosis have you in prospect? And are you steering so particularly well by yourself?"
>
> "Miserably! But I can dream. And the thought of a husband cuts me from any dreaming. It's all dead flat earth at once!" (400)

In fact, this conversation with Emma is Diana's turning point, when Emma's eloquent representations of Redworth's painful constancy are "an electrical bolt in [Diana's] bosom, shaking her from self-pity and shame to remorseful pity of the suffering lover" (400). Having come to view his suffering as romantic, then, she can first sympathize with and then be "kindled" by him.

Or it is possible to read Diana's transformation as the giving up of her dreams of romance and finding a more-mature satisfaction in a real rather than ideal man. Diana's earlier relationship with Percy Dacier aids this reading, since he has represented a passion for which she is willing, at least temporarily, to throw away everything else. The failure of this passion, one could argue, is what allows Diana to appreciate Redworth's humbler, and safer, charms. But if so, why does the novel emphasize Diana's "kindled" feelings for Redworth? These certainly fiddled persuasive harmonics for the novel's sensation-loving reviewer, who concluded his or her review this way:

> The interest heightens as the story and life grow older—no flagging attention for the reader—on he is impelled—the beauty of some soft saying, the lure of some passionate love scene, the lament of the woman that, by the confession of her love, she is humiliated—all bear him on, on resistless wings. (270)

This reader, at least, does not seem to view the novel's resolution as prosaic.

Still another option is to read in the novel's parting thought, given to Emma, a happy ending for eugenicists. Emma, watching the sunset and reflecting on Diana's honeymoon letters, thinks hopefully of the issue of their union. Those readers who find Meredith's writing perverse rather than ingenious are warned beforehand:

> Now the dear woman was really wedded, wedded and mated. Her letters breathed, in their own lively or thoughtful flow, of the perfect mating. Emma gazed into the depths of the waves of crimson, where brilliancy of colour came out of central heaven preternaturally near on earth, till one shade less brilliant seemed an ebbing away to boundless remoteness. Angelical and mortal mixed, making the glory overhead a sign of the close union of our human conditions with the ethereal and the psychically divined. Thence it grew that one thought in her breast became a desire for such extension of days as would give her the blessedness to clasp in her lap—if those kind heavens would grant it!—a child of the marriage of the two noblest of human souls, one the dearest; and so have proof at heart that her country and our earth are fruitful in the good, for a glowing future. (414)

Emma's affection for her friends is blended with eugenicist solicitude for her "race." Clearly, Diana and Redworth represent physical and mental superiority combined to produce equally superior children. It is fortuitous, then, that Diana has overcome her reservations about marriage in general and Redworth in particular.

But this final scene also becomes something else—Emma's reading of Diana's letters, in which Emma's own desires, like the sunset, color the horizon of possible meanings. For Emma, Diana's letters "breathe," but they breathe especially what she wants to hear. And thus the novel brings us back to its initial difficulty—interpretation. Emphasizing as it does the shiftiness of "historical" truth, the novel permits all of these various sentimental and realist readings to coexist at its conclusion. Diana's objections to the shackles of marriage are not negated by the kindling of her sexual desires, and just because Redworth and Diana are good breeding stock, it doesn't mean they aren't spiritually kindred lovers. But I would suggest one more layer to Diana's comic resolution: the romance that is threatened by marriage to Redworth is not, or not only, the prospect of a more-poetical lover, but also the fantasy of her own critical and political agency.

Diana's dearest vision of herself is, one might say, Meredith's dearest vision of Woman, which is articulated by Arabella Shore, following the publication of *The Egoist* in 1879, when she expresses the hope that Meredith might someday describe a more "perfect woman" and thus "by some clear illuminating ray cast from his own in some future work, aid in the great task of social regeneration" (147). Diana strives to be (and in many ways is) a woman of comic intelligence, capable of participating in the work of social regeneration. As Beer has pointed out, that Diana is a novelist, and one whose theory and practice of fiction closely approximate Meredith's own, suggests that Meredith staged his own cultural influence through his representation of hers. (*Meredith* 142–45). However, if Diana is Meredith's artistic proxy in the novel, then she bears witness to his willingness to turn the gaze of Comedy on himself, for Diana's attempts at social reform and progressive thinking are hopelessly enmeshed in sentiment. The narrator, for example, describes Diana and Emma's bluestocking-ish self-cultivation in this fashion:

> They were readers of books of all sorts, political, philosophical, economical, romantic; and they mixed the diverse readings in thought, after the fashion of the ardently youthful. Romance affected politics, transformed economy, irradiated philosophy. They discussed the knotty question, Why things were not *done,* the things being confessedly to do; and they cut the knot … O for a despot! The cry was for a beneficent despot, naturally: a large-minded benevolent despot. In short, a despot to obey their bidding. Thoughtful young people who think through the heart soon come to this conclusion. The heart is the beneficent despot they would be. He cures those miseries; he creates the novel harmony. He sees all difficulties through his own sanguine hues. (39)

The novel clearly treats the two women's intellectual endeavors with gentle satire here. They are compassionate, intelligent, but also foolishly romantic. The narrator tells us, however, that "by dint of reading solid writers, using the brains they possessed," they gradually learn that their reformist zeal may have selfish motives. They discover that "their particular impatience came perhaps of the earnest desire to get to a comfortable termination of the inquiry:—the heart aching for mankind sought a nest for itself" (39).

This passage suggests, on the one hand, in classic bildungsroman fashion, that in the course of the narrative Diana and Emma are moving beyond youthful idealism to a more-reflective wisdom—coming closer to disinterested Philosophy as they move away from sentimentalism. On the other hand, it shows Diana still clinging to her romance. Whereas Emma begins to acknowledge her own investments in their theories of reform,

> Diana had to be tugged to follow. She could not accept a "perhaps" that cast dubiousness on her disinterested championship. She protested a perfect certainty of the single aim of her heart outward. But she reflected …
>
> The discovery was reached, and even acknowledged, before she could persuade herself to swallow the repulsive truth. O self! self! self! are we eternally masking in a domino that reveals your hideous old face when we could be most positive we had escaped you? Eternally! the desolating answer knelled. Nevertheless the poor, the starving, the overtaxed in labour, *they* have a right to the cry of Now! now! They have; and if a cry could conduct us to the secret of aiding, healing, feeding, elevating them, we might swell the cry. As it is, we must lay it on our wits patiently to track and find the secret; and meantime do what the individual with his poor pittance can. A miserable contribution! sighed the girl. Old Self was perceived in the sigh. She was haunted. (39–40)

Diana's social critique is not negated by the recognition of her own sentimental investments, nor is her sentimentalism banished by her self-knowledge. The novel therefore suggests that the best that can be hoped for is a kind of ambivalent agency—neither wholly philosophical nor wholly sensational, but always, painfully, both. At its conclusion *Diana of the Crossways* leaves its readers where Diana is left at the end of this passage—patiently tracking our Philosophy and our social regeneration, but haunted nonetheless by regressive sentimentalism and egoism.

As critics have noted, Diana's gradual acceptance of Redworth is linked symbolically to the "red" of blood and fire that his name represents; he finally proposes "under the propitious flaming heavens," which Diana coyly refers to as the "seductions of 'Sol'" (394–95), and so on.[21] So, too, Emma's final "reflection" on Diana's marriage is blended with her contemplation of the "flaming heavens." But these passages, triumphant as they appear, must be linked to the failure of critical reflection described in the lines quoted above: "The heart is the beneficent despot they would be. He cures those miseries; he creates the novel harmony. He sees all difficulties through his own sanguine hues." Emma's conclusion, which is the novel's conclusion, creates a "novel harmony" that views the "difficulties" of the plot's resolution, both literally and figuratively, through "sanguine hues." Thus, even as the novel imagines itself doing the work of cultivating philosophical readers—and through them, civilization itself—it also shows that work unable to separate itself from romance.

The weight that is placed on the cultivation of the reader in *The Egoist* and *Diana*—wherein "cultivation" means both refinement of taste and careful husbandry of (human) resources—offers a way of reading *through* Meredith forward to modernism that suggests not a falling away of social and ethical engagement, but a development of the stance of the cultural critic whose very "disinterested" aesthetic critique signals his or her obligation to work for "social regeneration." If, as Arnold tells us in "The Function of Criticism," the free play of the mind on excellence and perfection allows the critic to produce not just rarified musings on the "great books" but a painfully succinct critique of society ("Wragg is in custody"), then may not that same critique be read in the epigrammatic moments in modernism that defy generic tradition and the reader's complacency? When, for example, the mad girl, Nancy, interjects "shuttlecocks" at the end of Ford Madox Ford's *The Good Soldier* or when Marlow refuses to repeat Kurtz's last words, "the Horror," to the blindly sentimental Intended in *Heart of Darkness,* the text's refusal of conventional resolution might be read as a commitment to the *cultivation* of readers. The phrase that I used to describe Meredith's vision of reading, "eugenics by way of aesthetics," alludes to the curious connections between aesthetic refinement and "racial" vigor in Victorian ideas of culture, but it also signifies, I would suggest, a phenomenon still current today: the critic's fantasy of omnipotence—that is, the belief that solely or primarily through the intellectual transmission from critical author (cultural authority) to student/reader may civilization evolve, paradigms shift, social horrors be addressed, and oppressive power structures be resisted. It is, without a doubt, a compelling vision of the "study of Arts in Letters." But as *Diana of the Crossways* demonstrates, this fantasy is no less susceptible to the pull of sentiment and sensation than the most romantic of love stories. And so the work of "Comedy" (or "Philosophy," or, one might posit, critical theory) must be to see in our own critical endeavors that "we are not so pretty as rose-pink, not so repulsive as dirty drab," but we are "soul[s] born active, wind-beaten, but ascending" (*Diana* 13).

CHAPTER FOUR

Conclusion: The Serious Work of Sensationalism

[Robert Audley] sat for hours smoking and thinking—troubled and gloomy thoughts making a dark shadow upon his moody face, which neither the brilliant light of the gas nor the red blaze of the fire could dispel.

Very late in the evening he rose from his chair, pushed away the table, wheeled his desk over to the fireplace, took out a sheet of foolscap, and dipped a pen in the ink …

"I shall draw up a record of all that has occurred between our going down to Essex and to-night, beginning at the very beginning."

He drew up the record in short detached sentences, which he numbered as he wrote.

It ran thus:—

"JOURNAL OF FACTS CONNECTED WITH THE DISAPPEARANCE OF GEORGE TALBOYS, INCLUSIVE OF FACTS WHICH HAVE NO APPARENT RELATION TO THAT CIRCUMSTANCE."

In spite of the troubled state of his mind he was rather inclined to be proud of the official appearance of this heading. He sat for some time looking at it with affection, and with the feather of his pen in his mouth. "Upon my word," he said "I begin to think I should have pursued my profession instead of dawdling my life away as I have done."

—Mary Elizabeth Braddon, *Lady Audley's Secret* (1862)

We labor under the delusion that power metaphors not only are locked into power but deliver analyses that are themselves powerful … And we settle into a power argument that is self-confirming, habitual, and flattering to all of us who want to beat up on others. Nothing wrong with that. The problem is that making power an unquestioned center limits the stories we can tell about our practices and the discursive practices we study—cultural, literary, multimedia.

—James Kincaid, "Resist Me, You Sweet Resistible You" (2003)

Every sensation narrative worth its salt gives its readers the big payoff—the revelation of a shocking secret, the deeply affecting portrayal of "high-impact" emotional energy with which to identify. If you have been following the narrative so far, you will suspect that the secret of *Problem Novels* has something to do with ambivalent agency and the vexed pleasures of reading, but like the secret in *No Name*, it was revealed at the beginning of the book. In any case, here is the satisfying conclusion, where all of the reader's labor will be rewarded. I want to end with two texts that address the literary critic's ambivalent agency and consider how these might shed light on the mystery of, and argue for a continued attachment to, sensational criticism for Victorian (and other literary) scholars.

The first quote above provides the penultimate clue. It turns out that even *Lady Audley's Secret*, the urtext of invisible disciplinary power, makes no secret of that power. If Robert Audley's detective work in *Lady Audley's Secret* can be distinguished by any particular characteristic, it is probably his angst-ridden musings on the seriousness of his task and on the limits of his own agency, which he imagines alternately as horribly empowered and as subject to external forces. His statement to his uncle provides an example of the former: "God forbid … that I should ever bring trouble upon such a noble heart as yours! God forbid that the lightest shadow of dishonour should ever fall upon your honoured head—least of all through any agency of mine!" (129). Conversely, he displays the latter attitude when he thinks to himself: "Whatever the mystery may be, it grows darker and thicker at every step; but I try in vain to draw back, or to stop short upon the road, for a stronger hand than my own is pointing the way to my lost friend's hidden grave" (167). This tension between instrumentality and agency is summed up in Robert's musing: "Why do I go on with this? … how pitiless I am, and how relentlessly I am carried on. It is not myself; it is the hand which is beckoning me further and further upon the dark road whose end I dare not dream of" (172). Here, as throughout the novel, Robert imagines himself with immense power over the lives of those he investigates, and yet he simultaneously conceives of his own will as being directed by disembodied "hands."[1]

His vacillation between fatalism and intense guilt underscores the seriousness of his task. His job is no fun. His responsibility to his missing friend, George Talboys, cannot be shirked, but carrying through with the investigation will make Robert responsible for ruining the lives of his family when he reveals the truth about his uncle's wife. This is why the pivotal scene that I quote above—in which Robert commits to paper all the particulars of the mystery—is an odd one. In it we see him, as usual, brooding on the mystery and his own role as detective. Yet the decision to write out the details of the situation that makes him so miserable produces a strange momentary pleasure as he contemplates his own agency with pride and affection. His pleasure, in addition to looking a little silly, seems in questionable taste given the novel's reiterations of the deadly seriousness of the work. Robert has just discovered what James Kincaid notes in "Resist Me, You Sweet Resistible You": it's fun to write "power stories," and even more fun to write oneself into the story as the "official" detective who gets to "beat up on others."

In his appraisal of critical practice after Foucault, Kincaid suggests that what he calls "power stories"—those interpretations that seek to reveal the workings of power—are prurient entertainment masquerading as serious work. Engaging in these narratives, observes Kincaid, allows critics to claim positions of resistance to power that offer "little victories for critics and scholars, but the fact that those victories are rigged, guaranteed in advance by the discursive formulas, takes away some of the sweetness" (1326). The stories that Kincaid identifies are what I have been calling sensational criticism. As I have argued, even recent work that critiques the "monolithic" power metaphor continues, notwithstanding that critique, to be structured by the same generic demands for sensational revelations. And it is precisely because of the "self-confirming" nature of these narratives that they continue to appeal to us, because the story is less about revealing things about the Victorians that were previously obscured than about secretly enjoying our own critical agency.

That we as critics enjoy a certain privilege in our interpretive work, however, hasn't been a secret, at least not since Nietzsche (author of the original power story) described the "will to interpret" in *On the Genealogy of Morals*:

> The cause of the origin of a thing and its eventual utility, its actual employment and place in a system of purposes, lie worlds apart; whatever exists, having somehow come into being, is again and again reinterpreted to new ends, taken over, transformed, and redirected by some power superior to it; all events in the organic world are a subduing, a *becoming master*, and all subduing and becoming

master involves a fresh interpretation, an adaptation through which any previous "meaning" and "purpose" are necessarily obscured or even obliterated. (77)

To make things mean is to wield power, however obscurely, and as Nietzsche shows, wielding power is fun.

Nor is it a secret that reading—even reading literary criticism—can be a naughty pleasure. I am taking it as a given that I am not the only one who gets a giddy thrill from reading and writing criticism. At least, if this is my perverse taste, it is one I share with Roland Barthes, who famously describes reading criticism in *The Pleasure of the Text*:

> How can we take pleasure in a reported pleasure? ... How can we read criticism? Only one way: since I am here a second-degree reader, I must shift my position: instead of agreeing to be the confidant of this critical pleasure—a sure way to miss it—I can make myself its voyeur: I observe clandestinely the pleasure of others, I enter perversion ... The writer's perversity (his pleasure in writing is *without function*), the doubled, the trebled, the infinite perversity of the critic and his reader. (17)

Yet the perverse fun of literary detective work seems to be stubbornly forgettable. We may notice with regret that other people are engaging in "Foucauldian melodrama" (Adams 859), but "we" ourselves engage in "extremely responsible and archivally informed" research (Jonah Siegel 310). Why is it that Victorian cultural studies, by and large, refuses to know its own sensational pleasures?

In *Annoying the Victorians* (1995) James Kincaid exhibits his (perverse) pleasures in literary scholarship for his readers' voyeuristic pleasure. This is the final clue. Throughout *Annoying the Victorians* Kincaid presents himself to his readers—like Robert Audley chewing on his feather pen and gazing at his handiwork "with affection"—in the act of enjoying his own critical agency. *Annoying the Victorians* is "problem criticism" in the same way that the novels in this study are problem novels, insofar as they all invite their readers to consider their investments in reading. Kincaid argues cogently for why his book does not simply produce readings of texts but attempts to denaturalize the methods by which we produce readings. His interpretations, he claims, will be "annoyingly wrong" (6). But this is because he is not trying to know the texts better, but to "use texts to suggest how it is they come to be known" (15). True to his word, he offers up his critical methods as comic display. For example, he writes this "review of scholarship" for his chapter on George Meredith's *Modern Love:*

> I have read everything ever written on Meredith's *Modern Love* ... When I say that I have read everything ever written on *Modern Love,* that of course doesn't mean that I have read *everything* ever written on *Modern Love,* or that I've read every word of what I have read or that I remember much of it. What I have done is consult the MLA bibliographies one by one ... starting with the latest and working backward until I had reached a point where enough was enough, the point where the sort of insights I had myself (and needed to be sure nobody who had had them before had published them) seemed very unlikely to pop up. (136)

Here, as throughout the book, Kincaid offers interpretations that both perform and parody our critical practices. He offers, indeed, an opportunity to "estimate [our] capacity for comic perception" by seeing our own habits rendered "somewhat ridiculous" (Meredith *Essay* 42).

In a 1996 review of Kincaid's book for *Criticism,* however, Antony Harrison is not disposed to "accept the correction" (42) proposed by Kincaid's comedy:

> *Annoying the Victorians* redoubles the pleasure of the primary text by adding to it the pleasure of sophisticated serio-comic criticism. What this book does not do, however, is add to our understanding of the Victorians or their culture or the ways in which the primary texts Kincaid treats operated in their Victorian contexts. This, of course, would be the job of historical criticism, which Kincaid not only eschews, but apparently despises. (167)

The job of historical criticism is huge, according to Harrison: "Simply stated, it regenerates a world. That is, it opens our eyes to the operations of literary texts within plausibly reconstructed historical fields of social and political particulars whose relations were previously unknown or opaque to us" (168). Harrison concludes that, despite how "delightful" Kincaid's book is, since historical criticism *does* do this work, and Kincaid doesn't, "it is difficult for me to envision the conclusion to [historical criticism] or to imagine its supersession—either by some as yet unformulated critical methodology or by the rejuvenation of some anterior critical compulsion. This would, needless to say, include Kincaid's serio-comical version of deconstruction" (169). In other words, Harrison cannot, finally, accept the book simply because it does what it says it will do and doesn't do what it says it won't do.

He argues against Kincaid's book on two registers. First, one might say that in describing Kincaid as "the Oscar Wilde of contemporary Victorian studies" (271), Harrison is arguing for genre preference, but his preference (realism) can't brook any other genres (decadence). It is hard to imagine a review of a novel or film arguing that the text fails because it isn't in the right genre. But somehow the stakes seem higher in literary criticism. The reason for this becomes clear in the second register of the Kincaid-Wilde comparison: seemingly Kincaid's criticism is perverse, nonproductive. Historical criticism, on the other hand, *is* productive: it creates knowledge; it is not perverse. "We" are not writing to satisfy a "critical compulsion" but to "regenerate a world."

Harrison's objection to Kincaid's book shows why Barthes' diagnosis of the critical perversion isn't quite right. As readers we are not voyeurs, watching the masturbatory pleasures of our fellow critics writing "without function." Rather, like Ruskin's woman in *Sesame and Lilies,* who is "taught to enter with her whole personality into the history she reads" (81), we are masochistically invested in our own agency. We "extend the limits of [our] sympathy with respect to that history which is for ever determined ... and to the contemporary calamity, which, were it but rightly mourned by [us], would recur no more hereafter" (81). Harrison's review illustrates one of the fundamental tropes of cultural studies criticism: that our work *is* work and that we undertake it earnestly and treat our mysteries with the seriousness they deserve. The prescriptions of genre look at least like methodological, and often like ethical, imperatives, and our pleasure must be disavowed, subsumed by the sense of our accountability. Doing it may be fun, but if you are doing it *for* fun, you are not doing it right. And if you are not doing it right, you are abjuring a solemn responsibility. This is the downside of indulging in a fantasy of critical omnipotence: one must feel a terrible responsibility and nagging sense of inadequacy.

In "Resist Me, You Sweet Resistible You," as in *Annoying the Victorians,* Kincaid invites us to sidestep the "responsibility" of literary criticism, offering instead a promising vision of a discipline undisciplined. Power stories are not productive, he argues, but restrictive. In their place he presents a manifesto for utopian plenitude:

> Story multipliers can find starting points by accepting what power stories deny. Alternative stories accept the possibility of the random and the uncaused, defy logic, and espouse an economy of surplus ... Story multipliers have no plots or long-term strategies, only local and disposable tactics, and they welcome all genres and genre mixtures, especially the impure. (1332)

If Foucauldian (and post-Foucauldian) scholarship tells the story of the detective-critic, imbued with exceptional observational and deductive powers, then Kincaid tells the tale of a world in which new species of critics flourish—a world of joyful contradiction and invention, where everyone gets to tell a story, and every story is different.

The problem with this utopia, to extend the metaphor of perversion, is that we're just not wired that way. You can't tell a masochist to be a foot fetishist and expect it to stick. The discipline of the academic profession is not undisciplined; it is, rather, extremely circumscribed, codified, exclusive, and even punitive. Entering into the discipline demands that we undergo years of training and submission to arcane rules and practices. Staying in it demands that we constantly renew our commitments to submit to its authority, through participation in annual reviews, third-year reviews, tenure reviews, peer reviews, book reviews, etc. Naturally, submitting to our discipline produces pleasure too. Why do it, else? But the pleasure is *in* the submission, specifically in the bind of agency that finds itself subjugated yet active, choosing its punishment, as it were. This is why, given the invitation to reject sensational criticism in favor of multiple, alternative stories, I find that I cling to the ambivalent agency that sensationalism can offer.

In *Lady Audley's Secret*, Robert's momentary pleasure is quickly superseded by the labor itself:

> When Robert Audley had completed this brief record, which he drew up with great deliberation, and with frequent pauses for reflection, alterations, and erasures, he sat for a long time contemplating the written page.
>
> At last he read it carefully over, stopping at some of the numbered paragraphs, and marking several of them with a penciled cross; then he folded the sheet of foolscap, went over to a cabinet on

the opposite side of the room, unlocked it, and placed the paper in
... a pigeonhole marked *Important*. (101)

Braddon's detailed description of the writing and editing process,
besides looking much like the academic writing process, reasserts
the seriousness of the detective work. Robert's work is *Important*. In
other words, Robert must forget his pleasure in his task in order to
reinvest in it so that his continued performance of it will be meaningful. [2] What is clear in the novel, though, is that Robert is right on
all counts: he is a pitiless agent of discipline; he is also subject to a
"stronger hand than [his] own" (167), and he is rewarded by a perverse pleasure in the contemplation of his subjection and his power.
What Robert is *not* is a dupe of discipline.

This, finally, is the story that *Problem Novels* seeks to tell: sensation criticism, like sensation novels, allows its readers and writers
to participate in fantasies of knowingness. But, as with the novels
in this study, sensationalism in literary studies need not signal our
hapless compliance with discipline. Besides telling us that old story
we love to hear—that if we apply ourselves seriously and responsi-
bly enough, we can know the Victorians inside and out—sensation
criticism also tells the story of our ambivalent professional selves.
Like Robert Audley, we are neither wholly powerful nor wholly subjugated. We too are agents of disciplinary power—not a monolithic,
all-encompassing panoptical power, it is true, but a vast institutional
network nonetheless. We too are subject to forces beyond our control.
Yet we can also, like Robert, enjoy moments of perverse pleasure in
the contemplation of our serious work.

NOTES

INTRODUCTION

1. As Goodlad herself writes: "Foucault's account of the Panopticon becomes, in effect, precisely the kind of flawed Marxist analysis he sought to avoid: an Althusserian-like theory in which reified 'Ideological State Apparatuses' (such as the Panopticon) directly dominate through subject constitution" (*Victorian* 11). And Ruth offers an interesting analysis of the current state of affairs of Victorian studies post-Foucault in her 2006 *Novel Professions.*

2. Thomas's work, along with Amanda Anderson's and Lauren Goodlad's, is one of the most frequently cited examples of the recuperation of liberal agency. For an interesting response to Anderson's and Thomas's recuperation of liberalism, see Elaine Hadley's "On a Darkling Plain."

3. I think one problem is that recent critiques of Foucault have tended to focus almost exclusively on *Discipline and Punish,* which, although extraordinarily influential in Victorian studies, was by no means the only important text. *The History of Sexuality* and *The Birth of the Clinic* in particular have been foundational, and in both of these Foucault is careful to avoid characterizing disciplinary power as totalizing or reified.

4. See also Winifred Hughes's *The Maniac in the Cellar.*

5. In his 2003 article "Resist Me, You Sweet Resistible You," Kincaid remarks: "Resistance is conceptualized nowadays within the metaphysics of power and has no currency outside that fashionable and gratuitous paranoia" (1326). Chow makes a similar point in her 2002 article "The Interruption of Referentiality," in which she writes: "An awareness of historical asymmetries of power, aggression, social antagonism, inequality of representation, and their like cannot simply be accomplished through an adherence to the nebulous concept of resistance and opposition" (185).

6. I am following a number of excellent studies over the past two and a half decades that have addressed real and figurative readers: Kate Flint's *The Woman Reader,* Patrick Brantlinger's *The Reading Lesson,* Ann Cvetkovich's *Mixed Feelings,* Audrey Jaffe's *Scenes of Sympathy,* Laurie Langbauer's *Novels of Everyday*

Life, Anita Levy's *Reproductive Urges,* Terry Lovell's *Consuming Fiction,* Jennifer Phegley's *Educating the Proper Woman Reader,* Garrett Stewart's *Dear Reader,* John Sutherland's *Victorian Fiction,* and Nicola Diane Thompson's *Reviewing Sex* are just a few. I consider my own work as taking up Kate Flint's point in *The Woman Reader* that "the practice of reading, at once pointing inwards and outwards, to the psychological and the socio-cultural, is an ideal site for the examination of Victorian ... and contemporary preoccupations: bodies, minds, and texts" (330).

7. A random selection of current books and book reviews, for instance, will show critics referring to scholarly projects in language much akin to the sensation/detective genre. For example, Ian Duncan's 2004 review of Patrick Brantlinger's *Dark Vanishings: Discourse on the Extinction of Primitive Races* says that Brantlinger "traces the early nineteenth-century consolidation of extinction discourse" (110). Similarly, Melissa Valiska Gregory writes in a 2004 review: "Kate Lawson and Lynn Shakinovsky investigate the obscure trace evidence of ... physical cruelty in *The Marked Body*" (689). Likewise, Ann McClintock conceives of Victorian imperialism this way in her 1995 book *Imperial Leather:* "Knowledge of the unknown world was mapped as a metaphysics of gender violence ... In these fantasies, the world is feminized and spatially spread for male exploration, then reassembled and deployed in the interests of massive imperial power" (23).

8. Adams is referring here to Karen Chase and Michael Levenson's *The Spectacle of Intimacy.*

9. In fact, having read Garrett's review before discovering Levine's book, I am describing my own experience.

10. This is quoted from the description of the Victorian Critical Interventions series on The Ohio State University Press's Web site: http://www.ohiostatepress. org/index.htm?/books/series%20pages/victorian%20critical.htm.

11. This is the launching point for Anderson's very elegant analysis, *The Powers of Distance.* Anderson moves beyond this critique of Foucauldian criticism to an unequivocal endorsement of critical detachment, or "reflective reason," within a model of procedural democracy that I find less convincing than her diagnosis of the blind spots in current critical theory. See *The Way We Argue Now* (2006).

12. See chapter 1 of Anderson's *The Way We Argue Now,* which also appeared in *Social Text* 54 (1998).

13. See Mary Lyndon Shanley's *Feminism, Marriage, and the Law in Victorian England, 1850–1895* for a good history of the Divorce, Infant Custody, and Married Women's Property acts. See also Tim Dolin's *Mistress of the House.* Susan Hamilton's collection *"Criminals, Idiots, Women and Minors"* offers a nice selection of primary texts and an introduction to women's involvement in the debates surrounding the issues grouped under the rubric of the "Woman Question."

CHAPTER 1

1. Similarly, in *Mixed Feelings,* Ann Cvetkovich maintains that the sensation novel's display of (particularly female) excessive affect works as a mechanism for producing, regulating, and containing that excess. According to Cvetkovich:

"The readers who are excited by the sensational lure of [the novels'] mysteries are provided with experiences of affect that are ultimately regulated and controlled" (7). See also, for example, Anthea Trodd's *Domestic Crime in the Victorian Novel*, in which she writes: "The narrative [of *Lady Audley's Secret*] is largely presented from Robert's point of view, and like *Basil* is a masculine inquiry into the mystery of domesticity. Robert, who initially endorses the domestic ideal Lady Audley so brilliantly impersonates, gradually discovers the sinister secrets which lie behind her realisation of this ideal" (105).

2. As Foucault asserts in *Discipline and Punish*: "Disciplinary power ... is exercised through its invisibility; at the same time it imposes on those whom it subjects a principle of compulsory visibility. In discipline it is the subjects who have to be seen. Their visibility assures the hold of the power that is being exercised over them. It is the fact of being constantly seen, of being able to always be seen, that maintains the disciplined individual in his subjection" (187).

3. I want to distinguish this from the role of the "suffering woman" that Ann Cvetkovich describes in *Mixed Feelings* as the heroine's passive submission to pain that is then converted into a sensationalized (eroticized) spectacle for the reader's delectation (100). For example, in *East Lynne* by Mrs. Henry Wood, Lady Isabel's pain becomes the reader's pleasure; she herself experiences no pleasure in it and, indeed, is powerless to avoid it. The conversion of pain to pleasure—in this model—is more a function of experiencing a sadistic enjoyment of someone else's unwilling suffering than it is of identifying with the self-designated sufferer. Conversely, the suffering in both *No Name* and *Armadale* is not only articulated, but is also often self-inflicted and deliberate.

4. See, for example Leo Bersani's account of the "shattering" of the self through masochism in *The Freudian Body*, or Carol Siegel's *Male Masochism*.

5. For a good critique of the problems in feminist theory with masochism, see Lynda Hart's analysis in *Between the Body and the Flesh*. See also Marianne Noble's *The Masochistic Pleasures of Sentimental Literature*. Noble's analysis of the eroticism of language in sentimental literature does an excellent job of addressing how, precisely, these texts participate in the production and proliferation of masochistic fantasies. However, she also tends to focus on female masochism as submission (albeit willing or at least complicit) to a specifically heterosexual, masculine, dominant regime.

6. F. Scott Scribner, in his article "Masochism and the Modern Ethical Ideal (1788–1887)," makes an interesting argument about what the masochistic contract does by turning away from the moral absolutism of Kantian ethics: "The masochistic contract offers an ethics insofar as it is an reenactment of the social contract, that refuses the totalizing gesture of the universal, while nevertheless offering a sensual ideal, grounded in the uniqueness of the situation and secured through the freely chosen law of the contract. Masoch's fiction is an intervention that affirms the particularity of an individual incarnation of an ideal as a model of social interaction, rather than the universality of the 'law' or the 'Good'" (79).

7. For a fascinating explication of Maine's *Ancient Law* in relation to Victorian sexual exchange see Kathy Psomiades's "Heterosexual Exchange and Other Victorian Fictions," in which she describes Maine's distinction between primitive society and "contemporary" Victorian society: "The world of individuals,

property, and contract that allows both capitalism and civilization to exist has a 'before' marked by the absence of all its distinguishing features. The primitive world is stationary, rather than progressive; one in which goods and people stay put, rather than circulate; a world of the group, rather than the individual; of the family, rather than the territorial state; of the unwritten law that is the parent's word, rather than the written law" (100).

8. In this I directly disagree with Massé, who writes: "Critics of the sublime school often find that a woman's suffering 'stands for' something else. As a feminist, I do not entertain this hypothesis or find it entertaining. When a woman is hurt ... the damage is not originally self-imposed: we must acknowledge that someone else strikes the first blow" (3).

9. Deborah Wynne offers a comprehensive examination of sensation novels, their serial publication, and critical reception in *The Sensation Novel and the Victorian Family Magazine.* See also Flint.

10. See, for example, Gesa Stedman's *Stemming the Torrent* for a discussion of the complicated articulations of the mind-body connection in Victorian psychological discourse. See also Athena Vrettos, Rebecca Stern, Jenny Bourne Taylor, Sally Shuttleworth, Ann Cvetkovich, Evelyn Ender, and Jane Wood. This is by no means a complete list. Most interestingly, in his 2004 article "Wave Theories and Affective Physiologies," Nicholas Dames suggests that nineteenth-century discussions of novel-reading convey a complex theory that "in its combination of physiological investigation with literary analysis, presents us with a vanished interdisciplinary formation, as well as an approach to the novel that might have renewed interest today as a precursor to an interdisciplinary theory of the reader, particularly the novel-reader" (207).

11. See Karen Odden's article "'Reading Coolly' in *John Marchmont's Legacy*" for an interesting account of how one sensation author imagined women reading simultaneously in two modes: "one in which she empathetically engages with the characters, and the other, in which she sustains self-awareness about herself as a reader" (23).

12. Ruskin differentiates between "the good book of the hour," in which group of pleasant and mildly useful texts the novel belongs, and the "good book of all time," in which the "greats" like Milton and Dante fall (32). The "good books of all time" are, of course, the ones to which one should submit oneself most thoroughly.

13. For an interesting account of the strangeness of Ruskin's rhetoric in *Sesame and Lilies,* see Seth Koven's "How the Victorians Read *Sesame and Lilies.*" See also Elizabeth Helsinger's essay "Authority and the Pleasures of Reading," in which she notes that the submission to the text that Ruskin promotes is not passive acquiescence, but rather a "complex mixture of obedience and freedom" (116).

14. Neither *No Name* nor *Armadale* have received the critical attention of *The Woman in White* or *The Moonstone,* but critics who do address them describe them in superlative terms (most convoluted, most perverse, most radical, etc.). Deirdre David, for example, contends in "Rewriting the Male Plot in Wilkie Collins's *No Name* (1862)" that "no [other] Collins novel ... so interestingly conflates resistance to dominant aesthetic and sexual ideologies as *No Name*" (34), although she also claims, rather inexplicably, that this resistance means that the novel "rattles

no nerves with sensational excitement" (35). Jenny Bourne Taylor, who reads the novel within discourses of evolution and psychology, does acknowledge the novel's sensationalism, remarking that as "Collins's most explicit treatment of the formation of social identity and of the cultural construction of femininity outside and inside the family," *No Name* "is a story of 'perversity.' … It is also a perverse story" (132).

15. Think, for example, of the suspicious reticence of *The Moonstone*'s heroine, Rachel Verinder, in regard to the disappearance of the diamond.

16. Magdalen's parents have pretended to be married while Mr. Vanstone is still married to a terrible, degenerate woman in Canada, so both Magdalen and her sister, Norah, are illegitimate. But when the first wife dies, while the daughters are in their teens, the parents marry immediately, unfortunately without realizing that this demands they make new wills so that the illegitimate daughters will not be disinherited. They both die before they can rectify their mistake.

17. Critics have tended to argue that the heroines of sensation novels are morally suspect, citing as the primary example Lady Audley. It seems to me, however, that at no time in the novel is she the heroine or protagonist. Rather, the amateur sleuth Robert Audley is the *hero,* and Lady Audley is the fascinating villainess. This may seem like a minor distinction, but it is crucial to understanding Collins's experimentation with the form of the sensation novel in his portrayal of Magdalen.

18. Indeed, under the law of coverture, this "death wish" was not just a psychological metaphor but a legal reality.

19. Magdalen, eager to marry Frank, sends her father on a last-minute trip to his lawyer to arrange her marriage settlement, and he is killed in an accident en route.

20. Caroline Reitz offers an interesting analysis of this vexed history of colonial violence and guilt in her article "Colonial 'Gwilt.'"

21. Interestingly, Victorian treatises on masochism suggested that schoolroom beatings could become "erotic flagellation," which would then produce in the beaten boys the desire to masturbate or, worse, the propensity for masochism in later life.

22. For an interesting discussion of the various significances with which Victorian culture imbued the racially ambiguous figure of the gypsy, see Deborah Epstein Nord's "'Marks of Race.'"

23. She disappears somewhere in the middle of the third book and never shows up again in person.

CHAPTER 2

1. See, for example, Henry James's review of *The Belton Estate:* "Mr. Trollope is a good observer; but he is literally nothing else … All his incidents are, if we may so express it, *empirical.* He has seen and heard every act and every speech that appears in his pages" (258).

2. For a detailed account of James's treatment of Trollope, see Elsie Michie's "The Odd Couple." See also Kincaid, *The Novels of Anthony Trollope.*

3. Trollope repeats these sentiments in *An Autobiography*, in his lectures "On the Higher Education of Women" (1868), and in his essay "On English Prose Fiction as a Rational Amusement" (1870). Although he was no great fan of Ruskin, this language also echoes Ruskin's criticism of the public in "Of Kings' Treasuries" for not recognizing that books are worth more than "munching and sparkling" (50)—that is, reading is *not* the same as consuming commodities like food and jewelry.

4. See also Andrew Miller's *Novels Behind Glass*, Rachel Bowlby's *Just Looking*, and Terry Lovell's *Consuming Fiction*, among others.

5. The special issue includes essays by Timothy Alborn, David Iztkowitz, Audrey Jaffe, Donna Loftus, and Mary Poovey.

6. This is a position that Mary Poovey elucidates in the introduction to her anthology, *The Financial System in Nineteenth-Century Britain*: "First, the lack of readily available information means that every piece of writing about finance in this period was an attempt to understand and interpret something that was only partially visible and constantly in a state of change. This means, in turn, that we should not read selections included here as straightforward descriptions. Even the entries taken from dictionaries, like McCulloch's *Dictionary of Commerce and Commercial Navigation*, need to be read as *interpretive descriptions*, which are informed both by their authors' proximity to existing sources of information and by their own theoretical and political positions on issues that were often highly controversial and imperfectly understood" (4–5).

7. Some recent scholarship also offers very interesting and nuanced accounts of the foundations of the credit economy and the production of belief in eighteenth-century economic theory. See, for example, Catherine Ingrassia's *Authorship, Commerce, and Gender in Early Eighteenth-Century England* (1998) and Gordon Bigelow's *Fiction, Famine, and the Rise of Economics in Victorian Britain and Ireland* (2003).

8. Similarly, much of the recent criticism exploring speculation and gambling casts the financial figure—Melmotte of Trollope's *The Way We Live Now* being the urexample—as the bogeyman of the realist novel. See, for example, J. Jeffrey Franklin's "The Victorian Discourse of Gambling" and his *Serious Play*, or Audrey Jaffe's "Trollope in the Stock Market."

9. In her book *Nineteenth-Century Literary Realism: Through the Looking Glass*, Katherine Kearns describes this kind of (psycho)analytical approach to Victorian realism: "Critics and marketing strategies … may thus promote realism as both fictional and true all at once: like the madman, incompetent as regards the really real, whatever the hermeneutic integrity of its visions, while, again like the madman, unimpeachable in its communication of a historical reality. Thus we see the paperback edition of *Adam Bede* using a fragment from the critical preface by Stephen Gill as promotion copy: 'Reading the novel,' says the cover, 'is a process of learning simultaneously about the world of Adam Bede and the world of *Adam Bede*.' In this marketing strategy, fictional realism shares a space with texts produced within the asylum … Realism is said to tell a (historical) truth despite itself even as it does not tell the truth" (7).

10. See Mary Poovey's introduction to *The Financial System in Nineteenth-Century Britain* for a good description of the legislation in the middle decades (1844–1862) that facilitated the growth of joint stock companies and individual investors (16–17).

11. David Itzkowitz, in his article "Fair Enterprise or Extravagant Specula-tion," offers a fascinating account of the rhetorical constructions of "legitimate" investing vs. morally suspect "speculation," which, he argues, became increas-ingly legitimized as it lost its connections to gambling in the latter decades of the nineteenth century. See also Audrey Jaffe's "Trollope in the Stock Market" for a discussion of the rhetorical distinction between investment and speculation.

12. For an interesting discussion of women and the stock market, see Andrew Miller's article "Subjectivity Ltd."

13. Trollope's paradoxical adherence to formal resolution and irresolution has been the crux of critical attention both from critics like Deborah Denenholz Morse and Jane Nardin, who want to consider how sympathetic or misogynist his portrayal of "real" women is, and from critics like Laurie Langbauer and Patrick Brantlinger who want to define the limits of his realism. As Morse notes, Trollope alters the "narrative conventions that embody the conventional view that feminine fulfillment lies only in love and marriage. The structure of the romantic courtship plot is broken in every novel, and there are elements that qualify the perfect closure in each novel's comic resolution" (3). See also George Levine's *The Realistic Imagination*, James Kincaid's *The Novels of Anthony Trollope*, and Christopher Herbert's "Trollope and the Fixity of Self," among many others, for accounts of the narrative tension in Trollope's novels.

14. In her 1854 *English Laws for Women in the Nineteenth Century*, a pamphlet calling for legislative reform, Norton compares her situation to the case of a slave in Ohio who sued his owner when the owner, who had contracted with the slave to allow him to buy his freedom, rescinded the contract after the money was paid:

> The case was argued with much ability; but at the close of the argument the judge decided for Mr Patton against Sam Norris, on this principle, that by the law of Ken-tucky "a slave cannot make a contract, nor can he have monies of his own." The con-tract, therefore, was null and void; and the money, though received and expended by the master, could not be held **legally** to have been paid ... I find, in the slave law of Kentucky, an exact parallel of the law of England for its married women; and in this passage in the life of the poor slave Sam Norris, an exact counterpart of what has lately occurred in my own.
>
> I, too, had a contract. My husband being desirous to raise money settled on me and my sons, to employ on his separate estate, and requiring my consent in writing before that could be done, gave me in exchange for such consent a written contract drawn up by a lawyer, and signed by that lawyer and himself. When he had obtained and employed the money he was desirous to raise, like Mr Patton of Virginia he resolved to "rescind the contract." When I, like the slave Norris, endeav-oured to struggle against this gross breach of faith,—I was informed that by the law of England, "a married woman could not make a contract, or have monies of her own." (19)

15. As is probably familiar to most readers, Cobbe is responding, as did numerous others (most famously W. R. Greg), to the 1851 census, which created a huge stir by showing a surfeit of single women in England. Greg's solution was to "export" single women to the colonies where there were more single

men. Trollope himself alludes to the problem in his 1868 lecture "On the Higher Education of Women": "It does not go smoothly with you all. There is not quite enough of money, not quite enough of feminine occupation,—not quite enough, perhaps, of husbands: and therefore ... you are all to be thrown into the labour market, and hustle and tustle for your bread amidst the rivalry of men. I do not myself think that you can improve your chances in life that way" (76).

16. This is a plot that recurs in different permutations in many Trollope novels, including *The Belton Estate* and *The Prime Minister*.

17. Critics have suggested that Miss Todd is, in fact, modeled after Frances Power Cobbe.

18. *Can You Forgive Her?* received quite a bit of positive praise from critics, even though, as Henry James notes in a review for the *Nation*, it includes "a certain amount of that inconceivably vulgar love-making between middle-aged persons by which 'Miss Mackenzie' was distinguished" (249). But even critics who applauded Trollope's portrayal of Lady Glencora and Plantagenet Palliser found Alice Vavasor hard to take.

19. Ironically, Henry James in his review of *Can You Forgive Her?* complains that George is not sensational enough, and having undertaken to represent a desperate character, Trollope should have gone all the way and had him kill someone or himself. (249–53)

20. We can gauge the magnitude of the tragedy threatened because a very similar one comes to fruition in *The Prime Minister* when Emily Wharton is not prevented from throwing herself away on Ferdinand Lopez, and only his eventual suicide (after his political and financial ruin) saves her and her family from permanent disgrace.

CHAPTER 3

1. McGlamery also offers an interesting Bakhtinian account of Meredith's difficult, yet instructive, preface in *Diana of the Crossways* in her article "In His Beginning, His Ends." See also Judith Wilt's *The Readable People of George Meredith*, a sensitive and generous reading of Meredith in relation to his readers.

2. For example, Carolyn Williams writes in "Natural Selection and Narrative Form in *The Egoist*": "Darwinism works as the touchstone of the novel's dramatic irony when it is falsely understood by the central character, the male Egoist Willoughby Patterne, and ... the true working of natural selection appears as a principle of narrative form, organizing the novel's plot, character development, and figurative language" (55). Williams offers one of the best and most detailed accounts of *The Egoist*'s Darwinism. Jonathan Smith and Patricia O'Hara also offer good explications of evolutionary rhetoric in the novel.

3. This is the gist of McGlamery's article "In His Beginnings, His Ends."

4. Caroline Norton was a renowned beauty and wit, a successful novelist and poet with influential friends in government and fashionable society. In 1826 she married George Norton, who was, by all accounts, an unintelligent, impecunious, and abusive husband. Their much-publicized custody, property, and divorce disputes began in 1836 when George Norton took their three sons from her. Under the law Caroline had no right to her children. George brought

a charge of "criminal conversation" against Caroline's friend Lord Melbourne. Lord Melbourne won the case, which exonerated Caroline of wrongdoing, but she lost custody of her children. And, under the current law, she was unable to sue for divorce. She mounted a campaign to give mothers custodial rights to their children, writing the pamphlet *A Plain Letter to the Lord Chancellor on the Infant Custody Bill* (1839), and the Infant Custody Act was passed in 1839. George and Caroline continued to have property disputes—she attempting to retain rights to her property and he attempting to eschew responsibility for her debts—over the next fourteen years. In a second lawsuit in 1853 George again cited Lord Melbourne's relationship with Caroline and won his freedom from financial responsibility for her debts. Caroline turned her attention to campaigning for revisions to the marriage and divorce laws. She wrote the pamphlets *English Laws for Women in the Nineteenth Century* (1854) and *A Letter to the Queen on Lord Chancellor Cranworth's Marriage and Divorce Bill* (1855). Caroline, unlike Meredith's heroine, was not able to remarry until after George died in 1877, when she was sixty-nine years old, and although this marriage to her longtime friend Sir William Stirling-Maxwell probably was happy, she was in poor health and died after only a few months. For a more-detailed discussion of the marriage laws and Caroline's campaigns to reform them, see Mary Shanley's *Feminism, Marriage, and the Law in Victorian England, 1850–1895*. See also Tim Dolin's *Mistress of the House.*

5. As such, the anxiety is one already inherent in Darwin's own accounts of sexual selection. Darwin's position on sexual selection in humans is notoriously slippery; he seems at times to argue that Woman in civilization no longer has the prerogative of choice, but at other times he maintains that civilized Woman has more freedom than her savage counterpart, and yet again he claims that savage Woman has more freedom to choose her mate than is at first apparent. However, vacillations notwithstanding, Darwin defines sexual selection thus in *Descent of Man:* "The sexual struggle is of two kinds; in the one it is between the individuals of the same sex, generally the male sex, in order to drive away or kill their rivals, the females remaining passive; whilst in the other, the struggle is likewise between the individuals of the same sex, in order to excite or charm those of the opposite sex, generally the females, which no longer remain passive, but select the more agreeable partners" (398).

I am indebted to Gillian Beer's *Darwin's Plots* for its groundbreaking discussion of the nuances of Darwin's theory of sexual selection. Rosemary Jann also offers an excellent account of Darwin's complicated rhetoric. As she explains: "By shifting his definition of instinctual sexual behavior in animals, he could project a version of the modern patriarchal family back across the border between animal and man. But this rhetorical move left him unable fully to explain what had subverted the sexual prerogatives of female animals or had produced the 'unnatural' behavior of the earliest savage cultures. The result was a narrative implicitly fragmented into rival discourses of continuity and rupture, progression and regression" (289).

6. This kind of dichotomy is perhaps most famously articulated by Andreas Huyssen in *After the Great Divide,* and although he himself problematizes the dichotomy, it is one that continues to inform discussions of the shift from Victorian to modern.

7. Woolf's essay collections feature dozens of essays that implicitly, and often explicitly, consider the question of "how to read." Aside from the obvious "How Should One Read a Book?," other essays such as "Reading," "Hours in a Library," "The Art of Fiction," and "Modern Fiction" (not to mention "The Novels of George Meredith" and "On Re-Reading Meredith") also speak seemingly to a readership that is not so "highbrow" as to be unable to benefit from instruction. Alison Pease offers a fascinating discussion of modernist articulations of the ethical dimensions of "the education of aesthetic reception" in "Readers with Bodies" (93).

8. Garrett Stewart remarks of Meredith's theory of Comedy that it "implies—in a teleological paradox—that true Comedy can only exist in the kind of highly evolved society that only true Comedy can help bring to maturity" (286).

9. As Amanda Anderson notes in *The Powers of Distance*: "Arnold saw the project of ethnology as subordinate to the larger, normative project of ideal culture for the individual, for the nation, and for humanity as a whole. The attempt to build the project of culture upon the findings of ethnology in fact stands at the heart of … *Culture and Anarchy*" (103–4). See also George Stocking's essay "Arnold, Tylor, and the Uses of Invention," in which he finds more similarities between Arnold and cultural anthropologist E. B. Tylor than are immediately visible, in that culture exists on a continuum for Tylor, such that it reaches its "full flowering" in civilization (as opposed to savagery or barbarism, earlier stages on the continuum). Thus, the "data" of European civilization are inherently superior to the data of a barbarous (non-European) society. See also Vincent Pecora's article "Arnoldian Ethnology" for an interesting rereading of Arnold's ethnographic tendencies.

10. For a good overview of eugenics in England and how Galton fits into the movement, see Peter Morton's *The Vital Science*.

11. Amanda Anderson argues, for example, that Arnold's emphasis on the study of perfection becomes a paradoxical insistence on what she calls "embodied universality," a particularized, "self-authorized" version of selfless and transcendent detachment. This emphasis on the particularized universal leads Anderson to suggest a reconsideration of Arnold in relation to Pater and Wilde—not antagonistic, as it is generally read, but similarly concerned with subjective experience. Regina Gagnier posits a similar claim in her article "The Law of Progress and the Ironies of Individualism in the Nineteenth Century," in which she argues that a shift in economic paradigms from a reproduction- and distribution-based model to one based on consumption and an "economics of choice, preference, and Taste" (325) parallels the shift in literary movements from the "high-Victorian [novel] plot of social relations" to the "individualism, psychologism and subjectivism" (315) of Aestheticism. Gagnier offers a socio-economic explanation for modernism's retreat from the marketplace and the social realm. Richard Kaye in *The Flirt's Tragedy* makes a similar argument, with Darwin rather than Arnold as the starting point of his Victorian-to-modern trajectory. He posits not just that "sexual selection's emergence as a scientific argument coincided with the rise of Paterian aestheticism," but that "Darwin's theory of male self-fashioning in *The Descent* provided an inadvertent basis for [the] Wildean credo … of sexuality emancipated from 'purposeful' predilections" (91–92).

12. Margaret Oliphant notes this dynamic, with bitter irony, in her 1880 review of *The Egoist*: "The author of *The Egoist* holds an exceptional position in literature. He is not a favourite with the multitude, but if that is any compensation, he is a favourite with people who are supposed to know much better than the multitude. His works come before us rarely; but when they do come, there is a little tremor of expectation in the air. The critics pull themselves up, the demigods of the newspapers are all on the alert. It is understood that here is something which, though in all probability caviare to the general, it will be a creditable thing, and a point in a man's favour to admire. Like Mr Rossetti's pictures, there is a certain ignorance, a certain want of capacity involved in the absence of appreciation. Not to know Mr Meredith is to argue yourself unknown" (236). This rhetorical dynamic is also ably described by Bill Bell in relation to Matthew Arnold in his article "Beyond the Death of the Author."

13. The language here is important. The "cultivation of aristocracy" plays with the two (of many) meanings of "culture": "good breeding" as in the refinement that comes of a high degree of civilization, and "good breeding" as in the judicious management of domestic animals—which are, in fact, at odds with one another. Clearly, the novel's portrayal of Willoughby suggests that both the refinement of culture and the process of sexual selection are thwarted by the cultivation of the aristocracy; Willoughby will indeed void the guarantee for the "noblest race of men to come."

14. Ann Cvetkovich says of *East Lynne* in *Mixed Feelings*: "*East Lynne* transforms a narrative of female transgression into a lavish story about female suffering, a suffering that seems to exceed any moral or didactic requirement that the heroine be punished for her sins" (100).

15. My own rhetorical use of "we" may seem intrusive here, but it is, I would suggest, precisely this uncomfortable inclusiveness that Meredith seeks to impose on his readers.

16. Jenni Calder is a notable exception. In *Women and Marriage in Victorian Fiction,* she remarks that "Laetitia is the ultimate victim" in the novel (187).

17. Robert Polhemus's reading of *The Egoist* in *The Comic Faith* does justice to the complexity and self-reflexivity of Meredith's idea of Comedy, which involves a "comic dialectic of egoism: his optimism, his belief in progress, and his challenge to each of us who reads it. We must 'consider' the egoist 'indulgently,' since he is part of us and we of him; we can't escape our kinship except by lying or obtuseness" (208).

18. Certainly from her inception onward Diana has inspired critical readings that seek to account for her psychological inconsistencies. Why does she marry Augustus Warwick? Why does she betray Dacier's political secret to the Press? As Mary Sturge Gretton writes in her 1907 study of Meredith's work: "The events and psychology of the book appear to us, not only not interwoven, but spun of materials so different in texture that they could not combine" (268). See Dolin, Boumelha, Beer, and McGlamery for contemporary examples. It is not my intention to enter into the debate here.

19. Vernon, imagining Clara wet with the rain, "clasp[s] the visionary little feet to warm them on his breast" (321). And after he finds her and takes her to the inn beside the train station to dry her shoes and stockings and makes her drink some of his hot brandy and water, Clara thinks of her exciting position:

"They were to drink out of the same glass; and she was to drink some of the infamous mixture; and she was in a kind of hotel alone with him; and he was drenched in running after her;—all this came of breaking loose for an hour" (326).

20. The relationship between Emma and Diana (or as Emma calls Diana, "her Tony") is emotionally intense and physically and verbally effusive, well beyond typical Victorian representations of female platonic relationships in novels, although the sisters' relationship in Christina Rossetti's "Goblin Market," with its overabundance of fruit juice and kissing, is close, as is the vampiric relationship in Sheridan Le Fanu's *Carmilla*. Boumelha addresses the complex relationship.

21. See, for example, Gillian Beer's *Meredith: A Change of Masks* and also Harvey Kerpneck's 1963 note "George Meredith, Sun-Worshipper, and Diana's Redworth."

CHAPTER 4

1. One should observe that when Robert meets Clara Talboys, George's sister, hers becomes the hand that commands him to investigate, but these particular passages occur before he meets her.

2. At this moment in the novel, the reader too reinvests in Robert Audley's serious work. The numbered list of clues is by now a common device of the detective story; the narrative pause allows the reader to make sure that he or she is tuned into the mystery thus far, in possession of all information necessary to solving it, and willing to continue reading. Indeed, one might say that the reader's pleasure is fueled by the painful seriousness with which Robert approaches his task. One imagines that *Lady Audley's Secret* would not engage its readers as effectively (and affectively) if Robert's pleasure in his "pitiless" investigation superseded his angst and not the other way around.

Adams, James Eli. "Recent Studies in the Nineteenth Century." *SEL: Studies in English Literature* 41, no. 4 (Autumn 2001): 827–79.

Alborn, Timothy. "The First Fund Managers: Life Insurance Bonuses in Victorian Britain." *Victorian Studies* 45, no. 1 (Autumn 2002): 65–92.

Anderson, Amanda. *The Powers of Distance: Cosmopolitanism and the Cultivation of Detachment.* Princeton, NJ: Princeton University Press, 2001.

———. "The Temptations of Aggrandized Agency: Feminist Histories and the Horizon of Modernity." *Victorian Studies* 43, no. 1 (2000): 43–65.

Anderson, Amanda, and Joseph Valente. Introduction. *Disciplinarity at the Fin de Siècle.* Edited by Amanda Anderson and Joseph Valente. Princeton, NJ: Princeton University Press, 2002. 1–15.

Armstrong, Nancy. *Desire and Domestic Fiction: A Political History of the Novel.* Oxford: Oxford University Press, 1987.

Arnold, Matthew. *Culture and Anarchy.* 1869. In Collini, *Culture and Anarchy,* 54–211.

———. "The Function of Criticism at the Present Time." 1864. In Collini, *Culture and Anarchy,* 26–51.

Austin, Alfred. "Our Novels: The Sensational School." *Temple Bar* XIX (July 1870): 410–24.

Aytoun, W. E. "The National Debt and the Stock Exchange." *Blackwood's Edinburgh Magazine* 66 (December 1849): 655–78.

Barthes, Roland. *The Pleasure of the Text.* Translated by Richard Miller. New York: Hill and Wang, 1975.

Beer, Gillian. *Darwin's Plots: Evolutionary Narrative in Darwin, George Eliot and Nineteenth-Century Fiction.* 2nd ed. London: Cambridge University Press, 2000.

———. *Meredith: A Change of Masks, a Study of the Novels.* London: Athlone, 1970.

———. "Meredith's Idea of Comedy: 1876–1880." *Nineteenth-Century Fiction* 20, no. 1 (1965): 165–76.

Bell, Bill. "Beyond the Death of the Author: Matthew Arnold's Two Audiences, 1888–1930." *Book History* 3 (2000): 155–65.

Bersani, Leo. *The Freudian Body.* New York: Columbia University Press, 1986.

Bigelow, Gordon. *Fiction, Famine, and the Rise of Economics in Victorian Britain and Ireland.* Cambridge: Cambridge University Press, 2003.

Bodichon, Barbara Leigh Smith. *A Brief Summary in Plain Language of the Most Important Laws Concerning Women; Together with a Few Observations Thereon.* London: John Chapman, 1854. *Victorian Women Writers Project,* 1997. <http://www.indiana.edu/ ~letrs/vwwp/bodichon/brieflaw.html>.

Boumelha, Penny. "'The Rattling of her Discourse and the Flapping of Her Dress': Meredith Writing the 'Women of the Future.'" *Feminist Criticism: Theory and Practice,* edited by Susan Sellers, Linda Hutcheon, and Paul Perron, 197–208. Theory/Culture 8. Toronto: University of Toronto Press, 1991.

Bowlby, Rachel. *Just Looking: Consumer Culture in Dreiser, Gissing and Zola.* New York: Routledge, 1985.

Braddon, Mary Elizabeth. *Lady Audley's Secret* 1862. New York: Oxford University Press, 1987.

Brantlinger, Patrick. *The Reading Lesson: The Threat of Mass Literacy in Nineteenth-Century British Fiction.* Bloomington: Indiana University Press, 1998.

———. "What is 'Sensational' about the 'Sensation Novel'?" In *Wilkie Collins,* edited by Lyn Pycket, 30–57. New York: St. Martin's, 1998.

Butler, Judith. *The Psychic Life of Power: Theories in Subjection.* Stanford: Stanford University Press, 1997.

Calder, Jenni. *Women and Marriage in Victorian Fiction.* London: Thames, 1976.

Review of *Can You Forgive Her?* by Anthony Trollope. *Spectator* (September 2, 1865): 978–79. In Smalley, *Trollope,* 245–48.

Cucullu, Lois. "Retailing the Female Intellectual." *Differences* 9, no. 2 (1998): 25–68.

Chow, Rey. "The Interruption of Referentiality: Poststructuralism and the Conundrum of Critical Multiculturalism." *South Atlantic Quarterly* 101, no. 1 (Winter 2002): 171–86.

Cobbe, Frances Power. "Criminals, Idiots, Women, and Minors." 1868. In Hamilton, *"Criminals, Idiots, Women, and Minors,"* 108–31.

———. "What Shall We Do with Our Old Maids?" 1862. In Hamilton, *"Criminals, Idiots, Women, and Minors,"* 85–107.

Collini, Stefan, ed. *Cultural and Anarchy and Other Writings.* London: Cambridge University Press, 1993.

Collins, Wilkie. *Armadale.* 1866. New York: Oxford University Press, 1989.

———. "The Art of Novel Writing." *The Gentleman's Magazine* (1872): 384–93. In Nadel, *Victorian Fiction.*

———. *The Moonstone.* 1868. London: Chancellor, 1994.

———. *No Name.* 1862. New York: Oxford University Press, 1986.

———. *The Woman in White.* 1860. New York: Bantam, 1980.

Cvetkovich, Ann. *Mixed Feelings: Feminism, Mass Culture, and Victorian Sensationalism.* New Brunswick: Rutgers University Press, 1992.

Dames, Nicholas. "Wave-Theories and Affective Physiologies: The Cognitive Strain in Victorian Novel Theories." *Victorian Studies* 46, no. 2 (Winter 2004): 206–16.

David, Deirdre. "Rewriting the Male Plot in Wilkie Collins's *No Name* (1862): Captain Wragge Orders an Omelette and Mrs. Wragge Goes into Custody."

    In *The New Nineteenth Century: Feminist Readings of Underread Victorian Fiction,* edited by Barbara Leah Harman and Susan Meyer, 33–44. New York: Garland, 1996.

Darwin, Charles. *The Descent of Man, and Selection in Relation to Sex.* 1871. Princeton, NJ: Princeton University Press, 1981.

Dawson, W. J. *Quest and Vision: Essays in Life and Literature.* 1892. 2nd ed. London: Hodder, 1894.

Deleuze, Gilles. "Coldness and Cruelty." In *Masochism.* Translated by Jean McNeill. New York: Zone, 1991. 9–138.

Review of *Diana of the Crossways,* by George Meredith. *Illustrated London News* (March 28, 1885). In Williams, *George Meredith,* 268–70.

———. *Pall Mall Gazette* (March 28, 1885). In Williams, *George Meredith,* 265–68.

Dolin, Tim. *Mistress of the House: Women of Property in the Victorian Novel.* Aldershot, England: Ashgate, 1997.

Duncan, Ian. Review of *Dark Vanishings: Discourse on the Extinction of Primitive Races,* by Patrick Brantlinger. *Victorian Studies* 47, no. 1 (2004): 110–11.

Review of *The Egoist,* by George Meredith. *Examiner* (November 1, 1879). In Williams, *George Meredith,* 202–5.

———. *Saturday Review* (November 15, 1879). In Williams, *George Meredith,* 218–22.

Ellis, Sarah Stickney. *Daughters of England: Their Position in Society, Character, and Responsibilities.* London: Fisher, Son & Co., 1842.

Ender, Evelyn. *Sexing the Mind: Nineteenth-Century Fictions of Hysteria.* Ithaca, NY: Cornell University Press, 1995.

Flint, Kate. *The Woman Reader, 1837–1914.* Oxford: Oxford University Press, 1993.

Foucault, Michel. *Discipline and Punish: The Birth of the Prison.* Translated by Alan Sheridan. New York: Vintage, 1979.

Franklin, J. Jeffrey. *Serious Play: The Cultural Form of the Nineteenth-Century Realist Novel.* Philadelphia: University of Pennsylvania Press, 1999.

———. "The Victorian Discourse of Gambling: Speculations on *Middlemarch* and *The Duke's Children.*" *ELH* 61, no. 4 (Winter 1994): 899–921.

Freud, Sigmund. "The Aetiology of Hysteria." 1896. In *The Freud Reader,* edited by Peter Gay, 96–111. New York: Norton, 1989.

———. "'A Child is Being Beaten': A Contribution to the Study of the Origin of Sexual Perversions." 1919. In Hanly, *Essential Papers,* 159–81.

———. "The Economic Problem of Masochism." 1924. In Hanly, *Essential Papers,* 274–85.

Gagnier, Regina. "The Law of Progress and the Ironies of Individualism in the Nineteenth Century." *New Literary History* 31 (2000): 315–36.

———. "Production, Reproduction, and Pleasure in Victorian Aesthetics and Economics." In *Victorian Sexual Dissidence,* edited by Richard Dellamora, 127–45. Chicago: University of Chicago Press, 1999.

Galton, Francis. *Hereditary Genius: An Inquiry into Its Laws and Consequences.* 1869. Cleveland, Ohio: Meridian, 1962.

Garrett, Peter. Review of *The Serious Pleasures of Suspense: Victorian Realism and Narrative Doubt,* by Caroline Levine. *The Modern Language Review* 100, no. 2 (April 1, 2005): 490–91.

Goodlad, Lauren M. E. "Beyond the Panopticon: Victorian Britain and the

Critical Imagination." *PMLA: Publications of the Modern Language Association of America* 118.3 (2003): 539–56.

———. *Victorian Literature and the Victorian State: Character and Government in a Liberal Society.* Baltimore: Johns Hopkins University Press, 2003.

Gregory, Melissa Valiska. Review of *The Marked Body: Domestic Violence in Mid-Nineteenth-Century Literature,* by Kate Lawson and Lynn Shakinovsky. *Victorian Studies* 46, no. 4 (2004): 688–90.

Gretton, Mary Sturge. *George Meredith: Novelist, Poet, Reformer, by M. Sturge Henderson.* 1907. Port Washington: Kennikat, 1972.

Hadley, Elaine. "On a Darkling Plain: Victorian Liberalism and the Fantasy of Agency." *Victorian Studies* 48, no. 1 (Autumn 2005): 92–102.

Hall, Donald E. *Fixing Patriarchy: Feminism and Mid-Victorian Male Novelists.* New York: New York University Press, 1996.

Hamilton, Susan, ed. *"Criminals, Idiots, Women, and Minors": Nineteenth-Century Writing by Women on Women.* Ontario: Broadview, 1995.

Handwerk, Gary J. "Blindness and Ironic Vision in *The Egoist.*" *Nineteenth-Century Fiction* 39, no. 2 (1984): 163–85.

Hanly, Margaret Ann Fitzpatrick, ed. *Essential Papers on Masochism.* New York: New York University Press, 1995.

Harrison, Antony. Review of *Annoying the Victorians,* by James Kincaid. *Criticism* 38, no. 1 (Winter 1996): 166–69.

Harrison, Frederic. *Studies in Early Victorian Literature.* London: Edward Arnold, 1895.

Hart, Lynda. *Between the Body and the Flesh: Performing Sadomasochism.* New York: Columbia University Press, 1998.

Helsinger, Elizabeth. "Authority, Desire, and the Pleasures of Reading." In Nord, *Sesame and Lilies,* 113–141.

Henderson, Archibald. *Interpreters of Life and the Modern Spirit.* 1911. Freeport: Books for Libraries, 1968.

Herbert, Christopher. "Trollope and the Fixity of the Self." *PMLA* 93, no. 2 (1978): 228–39.

Heyck, T. W. "From Men of Letters to Intellectuals: The Transformation of Intellectual Life in Nineteenth-Century England." *The Journal of British Studies* 20, no. 1 (Autumn 1980): 158–83.

Hoey, Frances Cashel. "The Novels of Mr. Anthony Trollope." *Dublin Review* n.s. 19, o.s. 71 (October 1872): 393–430.

Holbeach, Henry [W. B. Rands]. "The New Fiction." *Contemporary Review* 37 (February 1880): 247–62. In Olmstead, *A Victorian Art,* 151–66.

Hughes, Winifred. *The Maniac in the Cellar: Sensation Novels of the 1860s.* Princeton, NJ: Princeton University Press, 1980.

Huyssen, Andreas. *After the Great Divide: Modernism, Mass Culture, Postmodernism.* Bloomington: Indiana University Press, 1986.

Ingrassia, Catherine. *Authorship, Commerce, and Gender in Early Eighteenth-Century England: A Culture of Paper Credit.* Cambridge: Cambridge University Press, 1998.

Itzkowitz, David C. "Fair Enterprise or Extravagant Speculation: Investment, Speculation, and Gambling in Victorian England." *Victorian Studies* 45, no. 1 (Autumn 2002): 121–47.

Jaffe, Audrey. *Scenes of Sympathy: Identity and Representation in Victorian Fiction.* Ithaca, NY: Cornell University Press, 2000.

———. "Trollope in the Stock Market: Irrational Exuberance and *The Prime Minister.*" *Victorian Studies* 45, no. 1 (Autumn 2002): 45–64.

James, Henry. "The Art of Fiction." *Longman's Magazine* 4 (September 1884): 502–21. In Olmstead, *A Victorian Art,* 286–306.

———. Review of *The Belton Estate* by Anthony Trollope. *Nation* (New York) 4 January 1866: 21–22. In Smalley, *Trollope,* 254–58.

———. Review of *Can You Forgive Her?* by Anthony Trollope. *Nation* (New York) 28 September 1865: 409–10. In Smalley, *Trollope,* 249–53.

Jann, Rosemary. "Darwin and the Anthropologists: Sexual Selection and Its Discontents." *Victorian Studies* 37, no. 2 (1994): 287–306.

Jones, Wendy. "Feminism, Fiction, and Contract Theory: Trollope's *He Knew He Was Right.*" *Criticism* 36.3 (Summer 1994): 401–14.

Joyce, Simon. *Capital Offenses: Geographies of Class and Crime in Victorian London.* Charlottesville: University of Virginia Press, 2003.

Kaye, Richard A. *The Flirt's Tragedy: Desire without End in Victorian and Edwardian Fiction.* Charlottesville: University of Virginia Press, 2002.

Kearns, Katherine. *Nineteenth-Century Literary Realism: Through the Looking-Glass.* Cambridge: Cambridge University Press, 1996.

Kendrick, Walter. *The Novel-Machine: The Theory and Fiction of Anthony Trollope.* Baltimore: Johns Hopkins University Press, 1980.

Kerpneck, Harvey. "George Meredith, Sun-Worshipper, and Diana's Redworth." *Nineteenth-Century Fiction* 18, no. 1 (June 1963): 77–82.

Kincaid, James. *Annoying the Victorians.* New York: Routledge, 1995.

———. *The Novels of Anthony Trollope.* Oxford: Oxford University Press, 1977.

———. "Resist Me, You Sweet Resistible You." *PMLA: Publications of the Modern Language Association of America* 118, no. 5 (2003): 1325–33.

Koven, Seth. "How the Victorians Read *Sesame and Lilies.*" In Nord, *Sesame and Lilies,* 165–204.

Kucich, John. "Melancholy Magic: Masochism, Stevenson, Anti-Imperialism." *Nineteenth-Century Literature* 56, no. 3 (December 2001): 364–400.

———. "Olive Schreiner, Masochism, and Omnipotence: Strategies of a Preoedipal Politics." *Novel: A Forum on Fiction* 36, no. 1 (Fall 2002): 79–109.

Langbauer, Laurie. *Novels of Everyday Life: The Series in English Fiction, 1850–1930.* Ithaca, NY: Cornell University Press, 1999.

Levine, Caroline. *The Serious Pleasures of Suspense: Victorian Realism and Narrative Doubt.* Charlottesville: University of Virginia Press, 2003.

Levine, George. *The Realistic Imagination: English Fiction from Frankenstein to Lady Chatterley.* Chicago: University of Chicago Press, 1981.

Levy, Anita. *Reproductive Urges: Popular Novel-Reading, Sexuality, and the English Nation.* Philadelphia: University of Pennsylvania Press, 1999.

Lindner, Christoph. *Fictions of Commodity Culture: From the Victorian to the Postmodern.* Burlington, VT: Ashgate, 2003.

———. "Sexual Commerce in Trollope's Phineas Novels." *Philological Quarterly* 79.3 (2000): 343–63.

Loftus, Donna. "Capital and Community: Limited Liability and Attempts to Democratize the Market in Mid-Nineteenth-Century England." *Victorian*

Studies 45, no. 1 (Autumn 2002): 93–120.

Lovell, Terry. *Consuming Fiction*. New York: Verso, 1987.

Maine, Henry Sumner. *Ancient Law: Its Connection with the Early History of Society and Its Relation to Modern Ideas*. 1861. London: Routledge, 1910.

Massé, Michelle A. *In the Name of Love: Women, Masochism, and the Gothic*. Ithaca, NY: Cornell University Press, 1992.

Mayhew, Henry and John Binny. *The Criminal Prisons of London, and Scenes of Prison Life*. 1862. Reprint, New York: A. M. Kelly, 1968.

McClintock, Ann. *Imperial Leather: Race, Gender and Sexuality in the Colonial Contest*. New York: Routledge, 1995.

McGlamery, Gayla S. "In His Beginning, His Ends: The 'Preface' to Meredith's *Diana of the Crossways*." *Studies in the Novel* 23, no. 4 (Winter 1991): 470–89.

———. "'The Malady Afflicting England': *One of Our Conquerors* as Cautionary Tale." *Nineteenth-Century Literature* 46, no. 3 (1991): 327–50.

Meredith, George. *Diana of the Crossways*. 1885. New York: Norton, 1973.

———. *The Egoist*. 1879. New York: Penguin, 1968.

———. "An Essay on Comedy." 1877. In *Comedy*, edited by Wylie Sypher, 3–57. New York: Doubleday, 1956.

Michie, Elsie. "Buying Brains: Trollope, Oliphant, and Vulgar Victorian Commerce." *Victorian Studies* 44, no. 1 (2001): 77–97.

———. "The Odd Couple: Anthony Trollope and Henry James." *The Henry James Review* 27, no. 1 (2006): 10–23.

Miller, Andrew H. *Novels Behind Glass: Commodity Culture and Victorian Narrative*. Cambridge: Cambridge University Press, 1995.

———. "Recent Studies in the Nineteenth Century." *SEL: Studies in English Literature 1500–1900* 43, no. 4 (2003): 959–97.

———. "Subjectivity Ltd: The Discourse of Liability in the Joint Stock Companies of 1856 and Gaskell's *Cranford*." *English Literary History* 61, no. 1 (1994): 139–57.

Miller, D. A. *The Novel and the Police*. Berkeley and Los Angeles: University of California Press, 1988.

Review of *Miss Mackenzie*, by Anthony Trollope. *London Review* (April 8, 1865): 387. In Smalley, *Trollope*, 228.

———. *Saturday Review* (March 4, 1865): 263–65. In Smalley, *Trollope*, 215–21.

———. *The Times* (August 23, 1865): 13. In Smalley, *Trollope*, 238.

———. *Westminster Review* (July 1865): 282–85. In Smalley, *Trollope*, 231–32.

Monkhouse, C. Review of *Diana of the Crossways*, by George Meredith. *Saturday Review* (March 21, 1885). In Williams, *George Meredith*, 262–64.

Morse, Deborah Denenholz. *Women in Trollope's Palliser Novels*. Ann Arbor: UMI Research Press, 1987.

Morton, Peter. *The Vital Science: Biology and the Literary Imagination, 1860–1900*. London: Allen, 1984.

Nadel, Ira Bruce, ed. *Victorian Fiction: A Collection of Essays from the Period*. New York: Garland, 1986.

Nardin, Jane. *He Knew She Was Right: The Independent Woman in the Novels of Anthony Trollope*. Carbondale: Southern Illinois University Press, 1989.

Nietzsche, Friedrich. *On the Genealogy of Morals*. 1887. Edited by Walter Kaufmann. Translated by Walter Kaufmann and R. J. Hollingdale. New York:

Vintage, 1969.

Review of *No Name,* by Wilkie Collins. *The Reader* (January 3, 1863): 14–15. In Page, *Wilkie Collins: The Critical Heritage,* 134–36.

Noble, Marianne. *The Masochistic Pleasures of Sentimental Literature.* Princeton, NJ: Princeton University Press, 2000.

Nord, Deborah Epstein. "'Marks of Race': Gypsy Figures and Eccentric Femininity in Nineteenth-Century Women's Writing." *Victorian Studies* 41, no. 2 (Winter 1998): 189–210.

———, ed. *Sesame and Lilies.* By John Ruskin. 1865. Rethinking the Western Tradition. New Haven: Yale University Press, 2002.

Norton, Caroline. *English Laws for Women in the Nineteenth Century.* London, 1854. *Victorian Women Writer's Project.* 1996. <http://www.indiana.edu/~letrs/vwwp/norton/ englaw.html>.

Noyes, John K. *The Mastery of Submission: Inventions of Masochism.* Ithaca, NY: Cornell University Press, 1997.

Odden, Karen M. "'Reading Coolly' in *John Marchmont's Legacy:* Reconsidering M. E. Braddon's Legacy." *Studies in the Novel* 36, no. 1 (Spring 2004): 21–40.

O'Hara, Patricia. "Primitive Marriage, Civilized Marriage: Anthropology, Mythology, and *The Egoist.*" *Victorian Literature and Culture* 20 (1992): 1–24.

Oliphant, Margaret. Review of *The Egoist,* by George Meredith. *Blackwood's Edinburgh Magazine* cxxviii (September 1880). In Williams, *George Meredith,* 236–40.

———. "Novels." *Blackwood's Edinburgh Magazine* 94 (August 1863): 168–83.

Olmstead, John Charles, ed. *A Victorian Art of Fiction: Essays on the Novel in British Periodicals 1870–1900.* New York: Garland, 1979.

Page, Norman, ed. *Wilkie Collins: The Critical Heritage.* London: Routledge, 1974.

Pease, Allison. "Readers with Bodies: Modernist Criticism's Bridge across the Cultural Divide." *Modernism/Modernity* 7, no. 1 (2000): 77–97.

Pecora, Vincent P. "Arnoldian Ethnology." *Victorian Studies* 41, no. 3 (1998): 355–79.

Phegley, Jennifer. *Educating the Proper Woman Reader: Victorian Family Literary Magazines and the Cultural Health of the Nation.* Columbus: The Ohio State University Press, 2004.

Polhemus, Robert. *Comic Faith: The Great Tradition from Austen to Joyce.* Chicago: University of Chicago Press, 1980.

Poovey, Mary, ed. *The Financial System in Nineteenth-Century Britain.* Oxford: Oxford University Press, 2003.

———. *Uneven Developments: The Ideological Work of Gender in Mid-Victorian England.* Chicago: University of Chicago Press, 1988.

———. "Writing about Finance in Victorian England: Disclosure and Secrecy in the Culture of Investment." *Victorian Studies* 45, no. 1 (2002): 17–41.

Psomiades, Kathy Alexis. "Heterosexual Exchange and Other Victorian Fictions: *The Eustace Diamonds* and Victorian Anthropology." *Novel: A Forum on Fiction* 33, no. 1 (1999): 93–118.

"Recent Novels: Their Moral and Religious Teaching," *The London Quarterly Review* (1866): 100–24.

Reitz, Caroline. Review of *Capital Offenses: Geographies of Class and Crime in Victorian London,* by Simon Joyce. *Victorian Studies* 47, no. 1 (2004): 100–2.

———. "Colonial 'Gwilt': In and Around Wilkie Collins's *Armadale.*" *Victorian*

Periodicals Review 33, no. 1 (Spring 2000): 92–103.

———. *Detecting the Nation: Fictions of Detection and the Imperial Venture.* Columbus: The Ohio State University Press, 2004.

Roberts, Nancy. *Schools of Sympathy: Gender and Identification Through the Novel.* Montreal: McGill-Queen's University Press, 1997.

Roberts, Neil. *Meredith and the Novel.* New York: St. Martin's Press, 1997.

Ruskin, John. *Sesame and Lilies.* 1865. In Nord, *Sesame and Lilies*, 3–93.

Ruth, Jennifer. *Novel Professions: Interested Disinterest and the Making of the Professional in the Victorian Novel.* Columbus: The Ohio State University Press, 2006.

———. Review of *Victorian Literature and the Victorian State: Character and Governance in a Liberal Society*, by Lauren M. E. Goodlad. *Victorian Studies* 47, no. 1 (2004): 121–23.

Scribner, F. Scott. "Masochism and the Modern Ethical Ideal (1788–1887): Between Literary and Scientific Visibility." *Literature and Psychology* 48, nos. 1 & 2 (2002): 65–88.

Shand, Alexander I. "Mr. Anthony Trollope's Novels." *Edinburgh Review* 146 (October 1877): 455–88.

———. "Speculative Investments." In Poovey, *The Financial System in Nineteenth-Century Britain*, 173–200.

Shanley, Mary Lyndon. *Feminism, Marriage, and the Law in Victorian England, 1850–1895.* Princeton, NJ: Princeton University Press, 1989.

Sherman, Sandra. "Promises, Promises: Credit as Contested Metaphor in Early Capitalist Discourse." *Modern Philology* 94, no. 3 (February 1997): 327–49.

Shore, Arabella. "The Novels of George Meredith." *British Quarterly Review* 69 (April 1879): 411–25. In Olmstead, *A Victorian Art*, 133–47.

Shuttleworth, Sally. "'Preaching to the Nerves': Psychological Disorder in Sensation Fiction." In *A Question of Identity: Women, Science, and Literature*, edited by Marina Benjamin, 192–222. New Brunswick: Rutgers University Press, 1993.

Siegel, Carol. *Male Masochism: Modern Revisions of the Story of Love.* Bloomington: Indiana University Press, 1995.

Siegel, Jonah. Review of *The Culture of Property: The Crisis of Liberalism in Modern Britain*, by Jordanna Bailkin and *Cultivating the Victorians: Liberal Culture and the Aesthetic*, by David Wayne Thomas. *Victorian Studies* 47, no. 2 (Winter 2005): 309–11.

Smalley, Donald, ed. *Trollope: The Critical Heritage.* New York: Barnes, 1969.

Smith, Alexander. Review of *No Name*, by Wilkie Collins. *North British Review* (February 1863): 183–85. In Page, *Wilkie Collins: The Critical Heritage*, 140–42.

Smith, Jonathan. "'The Cock of Lordly Plume': Sexual Selection and *The Egoist*." *Nineteenth-Century Literature* 50, no. 1 (1995/1996): 51–77.

Starr, Elizabeth. "'Influencing the Moral Taste': Literary Work, Aesthetics, and Social Change in *Felix Holt, the Radical*." *Nineteenth-Century Literature* 56, no. 1 (2001): 52–75.

Stedman, Gesa. *Stemming the Torrent: Expression and Control in the Victorian Discourses on Emotion, 1830–1872.* Aldershot, England: Ashgate, 2002.

Stern, Rebecca. "'Personation' and 'Good Marking-Ink': Sanity, Performativity, and Biology in Victorian Sensation Fiction." *Nineteenth-Century Studies* 14 (2000): 35–62.

Stevenson, Richard. *The Experimental Impulse in George Meredith's Fiction*. Lewisburg, Pennsylvania: Bucknell University Press, 2004.

———. "Laetitia Dale and the Comic Spirit in *The Egoist*." *Nineteenth-Century Fiction* 26, no. 4 (1972): 406–18.

Stewart, Garrett. *Dear Reader: The Conscripted Audience in Nineteenth-Century British Fiction*. Baltimore: Johns Hopkins University Press, 1996.

Stewart, Maaja A. "The Country House Ideals in Meredith's *The Egoist*." *Nineteenth-Century Fiction* 32, no. 4 (1978): 420–41.

Stewart, Suzanne R. *Sublime Surrender: Male Masochism at the Fin-de-Siècle*. Ithaca, NY: Cornell University Press, 1998.

Stocking, George W. Jr. "Arnold, Tylor, and the Uses of Invention." In *Race, Culture, and Evolution: Essays in the History of Anthropology*, edited by George W. Stocking, Jr., 69–90. Chicago: University of Chicago Press, 1968.

Review of *The Struggles of Brown, Jones, and Robinson*, by Anthony Trollope. *Westminster Review* (July 1871): 574–75. In Smalley, *Trollope*, 138–39.

Sutherland, John. *Victorian Fiction: Writers, Publishers, Readers*. New York: St. Martin's, 1995.

———. "Wilkie Collins and the Origins of the Sensation Novel." In *Wilkie Collins to the Forefront: Some Reassessments*, edited by Nelson Smith and R. C. Terry, 75–90. AMS Studies in Nineteenth-Century Literature and Culture 1. New York: AMS, 1995.

Taylor, Jenny Bourne. *In the Secret Theatre of Home: Wilkie Collins, Sensation Narrative, and Nineteenth-Century Psychology*. New York: Routledge, 1988.

Thomas, David Wayne. *Cultivating Victorians: Liberal Culture and the Aesthetic*. Philadelphia: University of Pennsylvania Press, 2004.

Thoms, Peter. *Detection and Its Designs: Narrative and Power in Nineteenth-Century Detective Fiction*. Athens, Ohio: Ohio University Press, 1998.

Thompson, Nicola Diane. *Reviewing Sex: Gender and the Reception of Victorian Novels*. New York: New York University Press, 1996.

Trodd, Anthea. *Domestic Crime in the Victorian Novel*. New York: St. Martin's, 1989.

Trollope, Anthony. *An Autobiography*. 1883. New York: Penguin, 1993.

———. *The Belton Estate*. 1866. New York: Oxford University Press, 1986.

———. *Can You Forgive Her?* 1864. New York: Oxford University Press, 1982.

———. *Lady Anna*. 1874. New York: Oxford University Press, 1998.

———. *Miss Mackenzie*. 1865. New York: Penguin, 1993.

———. "Novel-Reading." *The Nineteenth Century* (January 1879): 24–43. In Nadel, *Victorian Fiction*.

———. "On English Prose Fiction as a Rational Amusement" (1870). In Parrish, *Four Lectures*, 94–124. London: Constable, 1938.

———. "On the Higher Education of Women" (1869). In Parrish, *Four Lectures*, 68–88. London: Constable, 1938.

———. *Phineas Finn*. 1869. New York: Penguin, 1985.

———. *The Prime Minister*. 1876. New York: Oxford University Press, 1983.

———. *The Struggles of Brown, Jones, and Robinson, by One of the Firm*. 1862. New York: Penguin, 1993.

———. *The Way We Live Now*. 1875. New York: Oxford University Press, 1982.

"The Uses of Fiction." *Tinsley's Magazine* (March 6, 1870): 180–85. In Olmstead,

A Victorian Art, 3–8.

Williams, Carolyn. "Natural Selection and Narrative Form in *The Egoist*." *Victorian Studies* 27, no. 1 (1983): 53–79.

Williams, Ioan M., ed. *George Meredith: The Critical Heritage*. New York: Routledge, 1995.

Wilt, Judith. *The Readable People of George Meredith*. Princeton, NJ: Princeton University Press, 1975.

Wood, Jane. *Passion and Pathology in Victorian Fiction*. Oxford: Oxford University Press, 2001.

Wood, Mrs. Henry. *East Lynne*. 1861. London: Everyman, 1994.

Woolf, Virginia. "How Should One Read a Book?" 1926. In *The Second Common Reader*, 258–70. New York: Harcourt, 1960.

———. "The Novels of George Meredith." 1928. In *Collected Essays*, Vol. 1, 224–32. London: Hogarth, 1980.

———. "On Re-Reading Meredith." 1918. In *Collected Essays*, Vol. 1, 233–37. London: Hogarth, 1980.

Wynne, Deborah. *The Sensation Novel and the Victorian Family Magazine*. London and Basingstoke: Palgrave, 2001.

Žižek, Slavoj. "The Masochistic Social Link." In *Perversion and the Social Relation*, edited by Molly Anne Rothenberg, Dennis Foster, and Slavoj Žižek, 112–25. Durham, NC: Duke University Press, 2003.

"sweetness and light." See *Culture and Anarchy* (Arnold)

Taylor, Jenny Bourne, 138n10, 138–39n14

Thomas, David Wayne, 3, 11, 34, 135n2

Thompson, Nicola Diane, 135–36n6

Thoms, Peter, 7

Trodd, Anthea, 136–37n1

Trollope, Anthony, 6, 11, 16, 18, 55–62, 64–90, 106, 122, 140n3, 140n8, 141n13, 141–42n15, 142n16, 142n17, 142n18, 142n19; reviews of, 11, 56–59, 71, 76, 83, 86, 89–90, 139n1, 142n18, 142n19. See also *Autobiography, An; Belton Estate, The; Can You Forgive Her?; Miss Mackenzie;* "Novel-Reading"; "On English Prose Fiction as a Rational Amusement"; "On the Higher Education of Women"; Palliser novels; *Phineas Finn* and *Phineas Redux; Prime Minister, The; Way We Live Now, The*

"Uses of Fiction, The" (Anonymous), 30–31

Victorian Critical Interventions book series, 13, 136n10

Victorian studies, field of, 1–14, 26, 60–64, 130–34. *See also* critic; criticism

Vrettos, Athena, 138n10

Way We Live Now, The (Trollope), 66, 87, 140n8

"What Shall We Do with Our Old Maids?" (Cobbe), 69, 75, 141–42n15

Williams, Carolyn, 114, 142n2

Wilt, Judith, 142n1

Woman in White, The (Collins), 5, 12, 35–36, 138–39n14

Woman Question, 15–16, 28, 69, 136n13

Wood, Jane, 138n10

Wood, Mrs. Henry, 25, 44, 110–12, 137n3, 145n14

Woolf, Virginia: on George Meredith, 91, 104–6; on reading, 96, 144n7. *See also* "How Should One Read a Book?"; "Novels of George Meredith, The"; "On Re-Reading George Meredith"

"Wragg is in custody." *See* "Function of Criticism at the Present Time, The" (Arnold)

Wynne, Deborah, 138n9

Žižek, Slavoj, 25–26, 29

VICTORIAN CRITICAL INTERVENTIONS
Donald E. Hall, Series Editor

Included in this series are provocative, theory-based forays into some of the most heated discussions in Victorian studies today, with the goal of redefining what we both know and do in this field.

*Lost Causes: Historical Consciousness
in Victorian Literature*
Jason B. Jones

The Old Story, with a Difference: Pickwick's Vision
Julian Wolfreys

*Novel Professions: Interested Disinterest and the Making
of the Professional in the Victorian Novel*
Jennifer Ruth

*Detecting the Nation: Fictions of
Detection and the Imperial Venture*
Caroline Reitz